STUDY GUIDE
Nancy P. Lynch, CPA, CMA
West Virginia University
Nancy C. Ruhe
West Virginia University

Financial Accounting: A Business Process Approach
Second Edition

Jane L. Reimers

PEARSON
Prentice
Hall

Upper Saddle River, New Jersey 07458

Acquisitions Editor: Steve Sartori
Product Development Manager: Ashley Santora
Production Editor: Carol Samet
Buyer: Michelle Klein

Pearson Prentice Hall^{TM} **is a trademark of Pearson Education, Inc.**

10 9 8 7 6 5 4 3 2 1

ISBN-13: 978-0-13-147399-7
ISBN-10:   0-13-147399-9

Table of Contents

CHAPTER 1
BUSINESS: WHAT'S IT ALL ABOUT?

Chapter Overview

This chapter will help you to understand what a business does, how it is organized, and how the financial statements reflect information about the business. Business events are classified as operating, investing, or financing activities. These business transactions are recorded in the business' information system and are summarized and presented in four basic financial statements. You should gain an understanding of who uses the information reflected in these financial statements. You will also be introduced to the concept of risk and the importance of ethics in business.

Chapter Highlights

1. A business provides goods or services either to make a profit (**for-profit** firm) or just to help people (**not-for-profit** organization). A business acquires inputs (capital, equipment, inventory, supplies, and labor) and pays for these goods and services. The business then adds value to these inputs, and creates and sells outputs (goods or services) to its customers and collects cash. The information about these activities is recorded in the company's information system.

2. There are four types of businesses:
(a) a **service** company does something of value for its customers, such as consulting;
(b) a **merchandising** company buys goods, adds value to them, and then sells them. A wholesale company sells to other companies and a retail company sells to customers who are the final consumers of the goods;
(c) a **manufacturing** company makes the goods it sells; and
(d) a **financial services** company adds value for its customers by providing monetary services such as lending, investing, insuring, or advising.

3. All businesses have owners, either individuals, groups of individuals or governments. There are three general forms of ownership:

- A **sole proprietorship** has only one owner. For tax and legal purposes, the owner and the business are considered one and the same. Profits from a sole proprietorship are taxed on the owner's individual income tax return. The owner is responsible for all debts and may have to use personal assets to pay business debts. Even though the law considers the owner and the business to be one, the financial records of the business must be kept separate from the owner's personal financial records. Financial information from a sole proprietorship is not available to the public.

- A **partnership** has two or more owners with the details of their rights and responsibilities specified in the partnership agreement. The law considers the partners and the business to be one, just as it does with the sole proprietorship. The partners are responsible for the business' legal liabilities and debt.

- A **corporation** has one or more owners, called **stockholders** or **shareholders** who own **shares of capital stock** in the corporation. It is considered a separate legal entity that is responsible for its own debts and pays its own taxes. The **Securities and Exchange Commission (SEC)** oversees the activities and financial reporting of corporations whose stock is publicly traded on a **stock exchange** (also called the **stock market**). Advantages of the corporate structure are (a) shareholders can own a small portion of the business, allowing them to diversify risk by investing in various other businesses, and (b) owners have limited liability. Disadvantages are (a) separation of management and ownership means that managers may make decisions that are not in an owner's best interest; and (b) corporate income is taxed twice, once on the corporation's own tax return and a second time on the individual owner's personal income tax return when he or she receives a distribution of corporate earnings (called **dividends**).

4. Each business transaction consists of an exchange whereby the company gets something by giving up something. These exchanges are recorded from the company's (not the owner's) point of view in the company's information system. These exchanges can be classified as operating, investing, or financing activities. Operating activities are transactions related to adding value to inputs (such as inventory) to create and sell outputs (goods or services) and then collecting cash from customers. Investing activities are related to buying and selling items the firm will use in its business for longer than a year, such as land, building, and equipment. Financing activities deal with how a business gets capital to fund its business. Financing activities include receiving money from owners in exchange for ownership (called **contributed capital**) and from borrowings in exchange for an IOU. The repayment of the borrowings or loan (**principal**) is also a financing activity. However, the cost of the borrowing, **interest**, is an operating activity.

5. The information system provides managers both financial and non-financial data to help make decisions and to plan, control and evaluate the operations of the business. The information system also provides the accounting records (commonly called the **books**) needed to prepare financial statements that are useful to investors, creditors, regulators, vendors and employees. The guidelines followed in preparing the financial statements are called **generally accepted accounting principles (GAAP),** which are set by the **Financial Accounting Standards Board (FASB)**. To help ensure the financial statements are accurate and reliable, the SEC requires companies whose stock is publicly traded to be audited by **Certified Public Accountants (CPA)**. In response to the many accounting scandals, in 2002 a new rule-setting group, the **Public Company Accounting Oversight Board (PCAOB),** was created by the **Sarbanes-Oxley Act** to oversee the auditing profession and public company audits. The information system is used for preparing reports required by other regulatory agencies such as the

Internal Revenue Service (IRS), the federal agency responsible for federal tax collection.

6. There are four financial statements: (a) balance sheet; (b) income statement; (c) statement of changes in shareholders' equity; and (d) statement of cash flows. A company's financial statements also include the **notes to the financial statements** (or footnotes), which describe the company's major accounting policies and provide other disclosures to help external users better understand the financial statements.

- The **balance sheet** shows the financial position at a particular point in time: Assets = Liabilities + Shareholders' equity. **Assets** (economic resources) are things of value owned by the business. **Liabilities** are amounts owed to others outside of the business (creditors). **Shareholders' equity** represents the owners' claim to the assets after the liabilities have been paid. Shareholders' equity is made up of **contributed capital** and **retained earnings** (earnings kept by the business). **Comparative balance sheets** show the balances at the beginning of the period and the end of the period.

- The **income statement** (also known as the statement of earnings, statement of operations, or profit and loss [P&L] statement) shows how well the company performed over a period of time. The period of time covered may be a month, quarter or **fiscal year** (a year in the life of a business that may or may not coincide with a calendar year). The income statement summarizes **revenues** (amounts the company has earned by providing goods or services) minus **expenses** (costs incurred in earning revenues), which equals **net income** (or net earnings). A net loss results if revenues are less than expenses. A **single-step income statement** lists revenues first and then groups all expenses together. A **multi-step income statement** starts with sales revenue first, then subtracts cost of goods sold to get a subtotal called gross profit on sales (or gross margin). Other operating revenues are added and expenses are deducted to arrive at the next subtotal, operating income. Lastly, non-operating items and taxes are listed to arrive at net income.

- The **statement of changes in shareholders' equity** shows the changes over a period of time in shareholders' equity. A corporation's **statement of changes in shareholders' equity** has two separate sections, one for contributed capital and one for retained earnings. Contributed capital increases if additional shares of common stock are sold. Retained earnings increases by the amount of income the company has earned (from the income statement) and decreases by any dividends paid to owners. Ending retained earnings (which will also show up on the balance sheet) equals beginning retained earnings plus net income (from the income statement) minus dividends. Retained earnings is **not** the same as cash.

$ The **statement of cash flows** summarizes the cash receipts and the cash disbursements during a period of time. The cash activities are classified into one of three sections, either operating activities, investing activities or financing activities. **Cash from operating activities** involve changes in cash from everyday routine activities such as collecting cash from customers and paying suppliers, employees and interest. **Cash from investing activities** involve changes in cash from buying or selling of long-term assets used in the business. **Cash from financing activities** involve changes in cash from contributions by owners and long-term loans.

7. All businesses face **risks** (potential injuries or losses) in order to earn rewards. **Controls** are designed to minimize or eliminate these risks. Management must always put good ethical behavior above appearing successful.

3

Featured Exercise

Part A: Show the effect of each of the following events on the accounting equation.

The following events took place in the month of May 2009.	Total Assets =	Total Liabilities +	Shareholder's equity	
			Contributed capital	Retained earnings
1	Henney Penney started a farm by taking $15,000 from her savings account and depositing it in a business checking account. The business, which is a corporation, HP Farms, Inc., gives her shares of stock.				
2	On May 1, the business borrowed $5,000 on a two-year, 12% note. One month's interest will be paid in cash on the last day of each month.				
3	The company paid Old McDonald $1,000 for one month's rent on a farm.				
4	The company paid $6,000 cash for chickens to be held in inventory.				
5	Sold 2/3 of the chickens to Pop Weasel for $9,000. a. Record the sale. b. Record the cost of goods sold.				
6	Paid Tom Piper $100 for cleaning the chicken coop.				
7	The company declared and paid a $1,000 dividend to Henney Penney, its owner.				
8	On May 31, paid $50 interest on the loan.				
	Totals				

Part B: Using the information from Part A, prepare the four financial statements for HP Farms, Inc.

Part C: Answer the following questions using Parts A and B. For each question below, fill in the correct dollar amount and circle the correct financial statement on which it appears using the following code:

IS for the income statement for the month ended May 31, 2009
BS for the balance sheet at May 31, 2009
SOCF for the statement of cash flows for the month ended May 31, 2009

a. Cash paid to suppliers for inventory of $_____ appears on the: **IS   BS   SOCF**

b. Inventory of $_____ appears on the: **IS   BS   SOCF**

c. Cost of goods sold of $_____ appears on the: **IS   BS   SOCF**

d. Total liabilities of $_____ appears on the: **IS   BS   SOCF**

e. Common stock of $_____ appears on the: **IS   BS   SOCF**

f. Net income of $_____ appears on the: **IS   BS   SOCF**

g. Retained earnings of $_____ appears on the: **IS   BS   SOCF**

h. Cash collected from customers of $_____ appears on the: **IS   BS   SOCF**

i. Sales of $_____ appears on the: **IS   BS   SOCF**

Solution

	Total Assets =	Total Liabilities +	Shareholder's equity	
			Contributed capital	Retained earnings
1	15,000 Cash		15,000 Common stock	
2	5,000 Cash	5,000 Notes payable		
3	(1,000) Cash			(1,000) Rent expense
4	6,000 Inventory (6,000) Cash			
5	9,000 Cash (4,000) Inventory			9,000 Sales (4,000) Cost of goods sold
6	(100) Cash			(100) Cleaning expense
7	(1,000) Cash			(1,000) Dividends
8	(50) Cash			(50) Interest expense
	22,850	5,000	15,000	2,850

Part B:

HP Farms, Inc
Income Statement
For the Month Ended May 31, 2009

Revenue		
Sales		$9,000
Expenses		
Cost of sales	$4,000	
Rent	1,000	
Cleaning	100	
Interest	50	
Total expenses		5,150
Net income		$3,850

HP Farms, Inc.
Statement of Changes in Shareholder's Equity
For the Month Ended May 31, 2009

Beginning contributed capital	$ 0	
Stock issued during the month	15,000	
Ending contributed capital		$15,000
Beginning retained earnings	0	
Net income for the month	3,850	
Dividends	(1,000)	
Ending retained earnings		2,850
Total shareholder's equity		$17,850

HP Farms, Inc. Statement of Cash Flows For the Month Ended May 31, 2009		
Cash from operating activities		
Cash collected from customers	$ 9,000	
Cash paid to vendors for chickens	(6,000)	
Cash paid for rent	(1,000)	
Cash paid for cleaning	(100)	
Cash paid for interest	(50)	
Total cash from operating activities		$ 1,850
Cash from investing activities		0
Cash from financing activities		
Issue of stock	15,000	
Proceeds from loan	5,000	
Dividends paid	(1,000)	
Total cash from financing activities		19,000
Net increase in cash		$20,850

HP Farms, Inc. Balance Sheet At May 31, 2009			
Assets		**Liabilities and shareholder's equity**	
Cash	$20,850	Note payable	$ 5,000
Inventory	2,000		
		Common stock	15,000
		Retained earnings	2,850
Total assets	$22,850	Total liabilities & shareholder's equity	$22,850

Part C:
a. Cash paid to suppliers for inventory of **$6,000** appears on the **SOCF**.
b. Inventory of **$2,000** appears on the **BS**.
c. Cost of goods sold of **$4,000** appears on the **IS**.
d. Total liabilities of **$5,000** appears on the **BS**.
e. Common stock of **$15,000** appears on the **BS**.
f. Net income of **$3,850** appears on the **IS**.
g. Retained earnings of **$2,850** appears on the **BS**.
h. Cash collected from customers of **$9,000** appears on the **SOCF**.
i. Sales of **$9,000** appears on the **IS**.

Review Questions and Exercises

Completion Statements

Fill in the blank(s) to complete each statement.

1. What all businesses have in common is that they provide their customers with something of _____.

2. A _____ company buys products and resells them to its customers.

3. A _____ is legally and financially separate from its owners.

4. The _____ oversees the activities and financial reporting of corporations whose stock is publicly traded.

5. In 2002 a new rule-setting group, the _____ was created by the **Sarbanes-Oxley Act** to oversee the auditing profession and public company audits.

6. Financial statements must be _____ (i.e., examined) by _____ who give an opinion on the fairness of the financial statements to ensure that they are accurate and reliable.

7. The _____ shows the financial position of a company at a particular point in time.

8. The _____ shows revenues minus expenses.

9. The _____ shows changes in contributed capital and retained earnings over a period of time.

10. All businesses face risks in order to earn rewards. _____ are designed to minimize or eliminate these risks.

True/False

Indicate whether each statement is true (T) or false (F).

_____1. The income statement shows the results of operations for a specific period of time.

_____2. Retained earnings is always equal to the cash balance of a company.

_____3. An asset is something of value that the company owns.

_____4. Retained earnings represents the amount owners have contributed to the business.

_____5. Dividends are a type of expense shown on the income statement.

_____6. Gross profit and operating income are sections in the statement of cash flows.

_____7. Net income appears on both the income statement and the statement of changes in shareholders' equity.

_____8. A company uses four financial statements to report its financial condition.

Multiple Choice

Select the best answer for each question.

_____1. Which of the following groups uses accounting information about a business organization?
   A. investors
   B. managers
   C. internal Revenue Service
   D. Securities and Exchange Commission
   E. all of these

_____2. Which of these businesses pays taxes on its income?
   A. corporation
   B. sole proprietorship
   C. partnership
   D. two of these
   E. all of these

_____3. How many of a company's four financial statements report information about the company over a specific period of time?
   A. one
   B. two
   C. three
   D. four
   E. none

_____ 4. Dividends are:
   A. the same as revenues.
   B. distributions to owners of a corporation.
   C. owners'contributions to the firm.
   D. another term for each partner's share of partnership income.
   E. shown on the income statement.

_____ 5. Which of the following is legally a separate entity from its owner?
   A. sole proprietorship
   B. partnership
   C. corporation
   D. two of these
   E. all three of these

_____ 6. What piece of information flows from the income statement to the statement of changes in shareholders' equity?
   A. revenues
   B. total expenses
   C. cash
   D. net income
   E. gross margin

_____ 7. In which of the following businesses are the owners' or owner's personal assets at risk when the business is unable pay its debts?
   A. sole proprietorship
   B. partnership
   C. corporation
   D. two of these
   E. all three of these

_____ 8. Which financial statement shows cash collected from customers?
   A. balance sheet
   B. income statement
   C. statement of changes in shareholders= equity
   D. statement of cash flows
   E. two or more of the above

_____ 9. Which of the following events increases retained earnings?
   A. owners' contributions
   B. purchase of inventory
   C. sale of inventory
   D. payment of rent
   E. payment of interest on a loan

_____10. Which of the following events decreases retained earnings?
  A. owners' contributions
  B. purchase of inventory
  C. purchase of land
  D. payment of dividends
  E. payment of the principal of a loan

Exercises

1. Identify each of the following as an asset, liability, or equity account by putting an "X" in the appropriate box. Only one box should be checked for each account.

Account Title	Asset	Liability	Shareholders' Equity
a. Notes payable			
b. Interest expense			
c. Sales revenue			
d. Cash			
e. Dividends			
f. Cost of goods sold			
g. Inventory			
h. Common stock			
i. Rent expense			

2. Put an "X" in the appropriate box to indicate the financial statement that is being described. Only one box should be checked for each item.

	Balance Sheet	Income Statement	Statement of Changes in Shareholders' Equity	Statement of Cash Flows
a. Reports the results of operations				
b. Reports the inflows and outflows of cash				
c. Reports assets, liabilities and shareholders' equity				
d. Reports amounts as of a specific point in time				
e. Reports the company's financial position				
f. Reports the economic resources owned and the claims to those resources				
g. Summarizes revenues and expenses				
h. Reports the activity in contributed capital and retained earnings for the period				

3. Use the following information to fill in the missing amounts A, B, C and D in the balance sheet below.

Tim's Wares, Inc. began its first year of operations by selling common stock for $6,000. During this first year, Tim's Wares earned revenues of $10,000. Expenses were $8,000. A cash dividend of $1,000 was paid to shareholders. At the end of the year, Tim's Wares' balance sheet looked like this:

Assets			Liabilities	
Cash	$ 1,000		Notes payable	$20,000
Accounts receivable	3,000		**Shareholders' equity**	
Inventory	2,000		Common stock	B
Land	A		Retained earnings	C
Total assets	$ 27,000		Total liabilities & shareholders' equity	D

4. For each of the transactions below, show the effect on the accounting equation by circling one item in each column.

a. Paid $50 for a newspaper advertisement announcing an upcoming sale.

Total assets	Total liabilities	Total shareholders' equity	
		Contributed capital	Retained earnings
Increase	Increase	Increase	Increase
Decrease	Decrease	Decrease	Decrease
No effect	No effect	No effect	No effect

b. Paid $10,000 for merchandise (inventory).

Total assets	Total liabilities	Total shareholders' equity	
		Contributed capital	Retained earnings
Increase	Increase	Increase	Increase
Decrease	Decrease	Decrease	Decrease
No effect	No effect	No effect	No effect

c. Sold $5,000 of merchandise to a customer. Record the sale.

Total assets	Total liabilities	Total shareholders' equity	
		Contributed capital	Retained earnings
Increase	Increase	Increase	Increase
Decrease	Decrease	Decrease	Decrease
No effect	No effect	No effect	No effect

d. The merchandise sold in c. above originally cost the company $3,000. Record the cost of goods sold.

Total assets	Total liabilities	Total shareholders' equity	
		Contributed capital	Retained earnings
Increase	Increase	Increase	Increase
Decrease	Decrease	Decrease	Decrease
No effect	No effect	No effect	No effect

5. Tim's Wares, Inc., had the following assets and liabilities at the beginning and end of 2009:

	Assets	Liabilities	Shareholders' equity
January 1, 2009	$300,000	$100,000	?
December 31, 2009	500,000	200,000	?

Compute net income for 2009 assuming no additional stock was issued and no dividends were paid.

Solutions to Review Questions and Exercises

Completion Statements

1. value
2. merchandising
3. corporation
4. Securities and Exchange Commission (SEC)
5. Public Company Accounting Oversight Board (PCAOB)
6. audited, certified public accountants (CPAs)
7. balance sheet
8. income statement
9. statement of changes in shareholders' (or stockholders' or owners') equity
10. Controls

True/False

1. True
2. False   Cash includes activities other than the collection of revenues and the payments of expenses and dividends. Cash activity includes many activities such as borrowing cash from creditors or paying cash for the purchase of land.
3. True
4. False   Contributed capital (or common stock) represents the amount owners have contributed to the business. Retained earnings represents the amounts earned and kept by the business.
5. False   Dividends are distributions of companies' profits to owners and are not expenses. Expenses are incurred to generate revenues; dividends do not generate revenues.
6. False   Gross profit (= sales – cost of goods sold) and operating income are subtotals found on a multi-step income statement.
7. True
8. True

Multiple Choice

1. E All of these groups and many others use accounting information.

2. A A corporation is considered a separate legal entity and thus must pay corporate income taxes on its profits. The shareholders must then pay individual income taxes on the dividends (or distributions of these profits). The law does not recognize sole proprietors or partners as separate from the business, so the owners pay taxes only on the profits of the business and not on the distributions of these profits.

3. C The income statement, statement of changes in shareholders' equity, and the statement of cash flows report business activities during the accounting period covered by these statements. The balance sheet shows the financial position of the company at a specific point in time; it does not show the activity during the period.

4. B Dividends are distributions (not contributions) of a corporation's (not partnership's) profit that are shown on the statement of changes of shareholders' equity and the statement of cash flows.

5. C A corporation is considered a separate legal entity. The law does not recognize sole proprietors or partners as separate from the business.

6. D The income statement shows net income (revenues minus expenses) for the period. Net income from the income statement is needed to determine the ending retained earnings balance (beginning retained earnings plus net income minus dividends) on the statement of changes in shareholders' equity.

7. D The owners of sole proprietorships and partnerships are responsible for all business debts and may have to use personal assets to pay the debts.

8. D Cash collected from customers is in the operating activities section of the statement of cash flows.

9. C Retained earnings is increased by net income. A sale increases net income and thus increases retained earnings. Although owners' contributions increase shareholders' equity, they increase contributed capital, not retained earnings.

10. D Dividends decrease retained earnings. Owners' contributions increase contributed capital; they do not decrease retained earnings. Purchases of inventory and land increase assets; they do not decrease retained earnings. Payment of the principal of a loan decreases liabilities, not retained earnings.

Exercises

1. Account Title	Asset	Liability	Shareholders' equity
a. Notes payable		X	
b. Interest expense			X
c. Sales revenue			X
d. Cash	X		
e. Dividends			X
f. Cost of goods sold			X
g. Inventory	X		
h. Common stock			X
i. Rent expense			X

2.	Balance Sheet	Income Statement	Statement of Changes in Shareholders' Equity	Statement of Cash Flows
a. Reports the results of operations		X		
b. Reports the inflows and outflows of cash				X
c. Reports assets, liabilities, and owners' equity	X			
d. Reports amounts as of a specific point in time	X			
e. Reports the company's financial position	X			
f. Reports the economic resources owned and the claims to those resources	X			
g. Summarizes revenues and expenses		X		
h. Reports the activity in contributed capital and retained earnings for the period			X	

3. First find the missing value for Land (A) which is $21,000 (= $27,000 - 1,000 - 3,000 - 2,000). Next, find the missing value for total liabilities and shareholders' equity (D) that is $27,000 (= total assets of $27,000). Common stock (B) is equal to the $6,000 for which common stock was sold. Finally, retained earnings (C) is equal to $1,000 [= beginning retained earnings ($0 since it is the first year of business) + net income ($2,000 = $10,000 - 8,000) minus dividends ($1,000)].

4. Total assets	Total liabilities	Total shareholders= equity	
		Contributed capital	Retained earnings
a. Decrease (50) Cash	No effect	No effect	Decrease (50) Advertising expense
b. No effect 10,000 Inventory (10,000) Cash	No effect	No effect	No effect
c. Increase 5,000 Cash	No effect	No effect	Increase 5,000 Sales revenue
d. Decrease (3,000) Inventory	No effect	No effect	Decrease (3,000) Cost of goods sold

5.	Assets	Liabilities	Shareholders' equity
January 1, 2009	$300,000	$100,000	**$200,000**
December 31, 2009	500,000	200,000	**300,000**

Shareholders' equity has increased by $100,000. Since there has been no change in contributed capital (no additional stock was issued) and there were no dividends during the year, the increase in retained earnings is due to net income equaling $100,000.

CHAPTER 2
QUALITIES OF ACCOUNTING INFORMATION

Chapter Overview

In Chapter 1, you were introduced to the four basic financial statements: the income statement; the balance sheet; the statement of changes in shareholders' equity; and the statement of cash flows. For these financial statements to be useful, the information in the statements must be relevant, reliable and prepared in a consistent way so that a user can compare the financial statements of one accounting period to other accounting periods, as well as compare one company's financial statements with other companies'. In Chapter 2, you will learn the qualities of financial statement information and the importance of accrual accounting in preparing the financial statements to ensure that they are useful to decision-makers.

Chapter Highlights

1. GAAP are the guidelines and rules currently set by the SEC and FASB. Financial statements prepared in accordance with these rules should result in information that is useful. To be useful the information must be relevant, reliable, comparable, and consistent. **Relevant** information is reported in a timely manner and should be significant enough to influence business decisions. **Reliable** information is accurate and must faithfully represent what it intends to convey. The information should possess **comparability** to allow meaningful comparisons of similar companies' financial statements. The rules should be consistently applied because **consistency** is needed so that decision-makers can compare the financial statements of one accounting period to other accounting periods. For instance, **profit** (revenues minus expenses) for a period should be determined in a consistent manner with a prior period's profit so meaningful comparisons can be made.

GAAP provide guidance for measuring and reporting the elements of the financial statements. GAAP require companies to keep the owners' personal financial records separate from the

businesses'. This is called the **separate-entity assumption**. The **monetary-unit assumption** requires the elements to be measured in dollars. The **time-period assumption** suggests that the life of a company and its performance can be divided into time periods. The items on the financial statements are to be recorded at cost, referred to as the **historical-cost principle**. The justification for reporting items at cost rather than their current values is that cost is reliable (i.e., unbiased and verifiable). The **going-concern assumption** assumes that a company is not going to go out of business and sell off all of its assets. Thus, it is relevant to report values at cost since one does not need to know what items are worth currently if they are not going to be sold in the immediate future. Asset values are more reliable and objective if they are reported at cost and **not revalued** to what the company *thinks* they may be worth. Certain assets are, however, revalued using an objective method of revaluing (more on that in later chapters).

Two constraints apply to the preparing of financial statements. GAAP must be followed when an amount is considered material, that is, large enough to affect someone's interpretation or decision. The **materiality** principle allows companies to report immaterial (insignificant) items in the most cost-effective manner, even if it means a departure from GAAP. The other constraint is **conservatism**. Accountants should select the accounting treatment that will be least likely to overstate income or overstate assets.

2. A complete set of financial statements includes (a) the income statement (also called the statement of operations), (b) the balance sheet (also called the statement of financial position), (c) the statement of changes in shareholders' (or owners') equity, (d) the statement of cash flows, and (e) notes to the financial statements (sometimes called footnotes). Before financial statements are prepared, the company must be sure to adjust all account balances to reflect accurate amounts. This process is called **adjusting the books**.

3. The income statement is prepared first. It lists the revenues earned minus all the expenses incurred in generating revenue during the accounting period covered by the statement. Revenues increase and expenses decrease retained earnings.

Assets	Liabilities	Shareholders' equity	
		Contributed capital	Retained earnings
			+ Revenues
			- Expenses

Net income (sometimes called the bottom line) is the difference between the revenues (or sales) and the expenses (such as cost of goods sold, advertising expense, etc.).

- Revenue equals the dollar amounts of goods or services delivered during the period; it does not reflect the amount of cash received during the period. Some sales may have been made **on account** (or on credit). The statement of cash flows will show the amount of cash collected from customers during the period. **Accounts receivable**, an asset on the balance sheet, will show the amount that has not yet been collected from customers. Thus, the three statements tell three important pieces of information about the sales and collections: 1) the income statement shows the dollar amount of goods or services delivered (revenue), 2) the statement of cash flows shows the amount of cash received, and 3) the balance sheet links the two and shows the amount of revenue not yet collected (accounts receivable).

- Expenses are matched with the revenues they helped to generate. Expenses equal the dollar amount of goods or services consumed (used) during the period; they do not reflect the amount of cash paid during the period. Some expenses may have been paid for in advance (*i.e.*, in a previous accounting period). **Prepaids**, an asset on the balance sheet, will show the amount that has been paid for in advance but not used. Some expenses may not be paid for until a later accounting period. **Payables**, which are liabilities on the balance

sheet, show the amounts still owed on items that may have been consumed (used) during the period. The statement of cash flows will show the amount paid during the period. The income statement shows the dollar amount of goods or services consumed (expenses), the statement of cash flows shows the amount of cash paid, and the balance sheet links the two and shows the amount of expenses not yet paid (payables) or the amount paid for in advance (prepaids).

4. Net income from the income statement is needed to prepare the statement of changes in shareholders' equity. This statement shows the changes over a period of time in shareholders' equity caused by the following:

Assets	Liabilities	Shareholders' equity	
		Contributed capital	Retained earnings
		+ Common stock	
			+ Net income
			- Dividends

5. The balance sheet is prepared by calculating and summarizing the balance of each asset, liability, and shareholders' equity account as of the balance sheet date. The balance sheet balances because Assets = Liabilities + Shareholders' equity. The ending balance for each account is calculated by taking its beginning balance (*i.e.*, its balance at the end of the previous accounting period) and adding the changes in the account during the period.

6. The statement of cash flows shows every cash collection and every cash payment. Each cash transaction is classified as one of three types: operating, investing, or financing.

7. The notes to the financial statements are a crucial part of the financial statements. The **full-disclosure principle** requires companies to disclose any circumstances and events that would make a difference to the users of the financial statements.

8. The assets, items of value that will provide future benefit, are listed in order of **liquidity** (the relative quickness with which each asset is to be turned into cash or used). A **classified balance sheet** categorizes assets (and liabilities) as either current or noncurrent. **Current assets**, which will be turned into cash or used up within the year, are listed first, typically in this order:

- Cash, which is the most liquid asset.

- Short-term investments are investments made with the company's excess cash for example, when a company pays cash to buy stock in another company.

- **Accounts receivable**, often listed next, represents the amounts owed by customers from credit sales.

- **Inventory** is merchandise the company has available to sell.

- **Prepaids** represent payments made in advance for items that will provide future benefit--for example, prepaid insurance.

Noncurrent (or **long-term**) **assets** will last for more than one year and are listed below current assets.

9. Liabilities are obligations a company owes and, like assets, are separated into current and noncurrent sections on a formal classified balance sheet. **Current liabilities** will be settled (or paid off) within the year.

- An example of a current liability is **Accounts payable,** which is the amount owed to vendors for the purchase of inventory on account.

- Other payables are amounts owed to others for services or goods other than inventory.

Noncurrent (or **long-term**) **liabilities** are the obligations that will not be satisfied within the year and are listed below current liabilities.

10. **Equity** is the last section of the balance sheet and represents the shareholders' claims to the assets. Shareholders' equity for a corporation is separated into **contributed capital** (also known as **paid-in capital** or investments by owners) and **retained earnings** (capital earned and kept by the company). The balance sheet of a sole proprietorship or partnership shows the two sections, investments by owners and earned capital, combined as one, called **capital**.

11. For financial statements to be relevant to users, GAAP requires them to reflect the economic substance of the company's transactions. **Accrual accounting** requires revenue and expense be recorded when in substance the revenue is earned and the expense is incurred, regardless of whether cash has changed hands. Often revenues and expenses are reported in a different accounting period than when the cash is received or paid. **Accruals** exist when the action (revenue or expense) comes before the cash (receipt or payment). **Deferrals** exist when the cash comes before the action.

- The rule for recording revenue is the **revenue-recognition principle**. Revenue is **recognized** (*i.e.*, reported) on the income statement in the period it is **earned**, even if cash has not been received or was received in advance. For example, when a company delivers a product to a customer on account, the revenue should be recorded when the product is delivered. In substance, the company has completed its side of the bargain and should be able to reflect this revenue on its income statement. The company should not have to wait until later when the cash is finally received.

- The rule for recording expenses is the **matching principle**. Expenses are to be recorded (matched) on the income statement in the same period as the revenue they helped to generate, even if cash has not been paid or was paid in advance. For example, when a product is delivered to a customer, the expense of the product (cost of goods sold) should be matched with the related revenue (sales), regardless of whether the company has paid for the inventory in advance or still owes for the inventory.

12. In contrast to accrual-basis accounting, **cash-basis accounting** records revenue only when cash is received and expenses only when cash is paid. It often ignores the substance of the transaction and can result in manipulation and inconsistencies in the timing of revenues and expenses. It is not an acceptable method of accounting under GAAP.

13. Financial statements provide information about the risk of investing in a company. **Risk** is the uncertainty associated with the amount and timing of future returns. If the risk is considered high, then the investor expects a higher return. Investing as an owner is riskier than investing as a creditor because a company has a legal obligation to pay its creditors before its owners. Thus, an owner expects a higher return than a creditor via dividends and an increase in the stock price. A creditor can only expect to receive the agreed upon interest and repayment of the principal.

14. The **current ratio** equals current assets divided by current liabilities. It is a measure of a company's short-term **liquidity**, or ability to meet its short-term obligations.

15. There are three types of controls a company can use to minimize the risk of errors in the accounting system. **Preventive controls** such as keeping cash locked up are designed to prevent an error or irregularity (an intentional error). **Detective controls** such as preparing cash reconciliations are designed to find an error or irregularity. **Corrective controls** such as denying future credit to slow paying or non-paying customers are designed to fix errors.

Featured Exercise

Part A: Show the effect of the following events on the accounting equations for each of the childcare companies, Tom's Tots, Inc. and Tiny Tim's, Inc.

Tom's Tots, Inc.		Assets =	Liabilities +	Shareholder's equity	
				Contributed capital	Retained earnings
	May 1, 2008 balances	900 Cash 600 Prepaid insurance 200 Supplies	400 Note payable	700 Common stock	600 Retained earnings
1	Cares for 5 children for a fee of $300 per month for each child; collects cash.				
2	Pays off the entire loan plus $4 interest				
3	Pays $500 for May's rent				
4	Determines that 1/3 of the insurance is used up				
5	On May 31, only $50 of supplies are left				

Tiny Tim's, Inc.		Assets =	Liabilities +	Shareholder's equity	
				Contributed capital	Retained earnings
	May 1, 2008 balances	900 Cash 600 Prepaid insurance 200 Supplies	400 Note payable	700 Common stock	600 Retained earnings
1	Cares for 5 children for a fee of $300 per month for each child, to be collected in June				
2	Pays $4 interest on the loan				
3	Pays $500 for May's rent				
4	Determines that 1/3 of the insurance is used up				
5	On May 31, only $50 of supplies are left				

Part B: Using the information from Part A, prepare the four financial statements for both companies.

Tom's Tots, Inc. Income Statement For the Month Ended May 31, 2008	Tiny Tim's, Inc. Income Statement For the Month Ended May 31, 2008

Tom's Tots, Inc. Statement of Changes in Shareholder's Equity For the Month Ended May 31, 2008	Tiny Tim's, Inc. Statement of Changes in Shareholder's Equity For the Month Ended May 31, 2008

Tom's Tots, Inc. Balance Sheet May 31, 2008	Tiny Tim's, Inc. Balance Sheet May 31, 2008

Tom's Tots, Inc. Statement of Cash Flows For the Month Ended May 31, 2008	Tiny Tim's, Inc. Statement of Cash Flows For the Month Ended May 31, 2008

Part C: Answer the following questions using Parts A and B.

1. Are Tom's Tots and Tiny Tim's sole proprietorships, partnerships or corporations? How can you tell?

2. Who should expect a higher return, the creditor who lent Tiny Tim's $400 or Tim, the owner of Tiny Tim's? Why?

3. Is Tom allowed to include his personal rent expense in Tom's Tots' income statement? Why or why not?

4. Which assumption requires that the items in the financial statements be measured in money, not inches or number of kids?

5. Tom's Tots' supplies on hand, which were bought at deeply discounted prices, would cost $75 to replace as of May 31, 2008. Should Tom's Tots revalue the supplies to $75 on its financial statements? Why or why not?

6. Describe and explain the revenue-recognition principle using the transactions from Tiny Tim's during the month ended May 31, 2008.

7. Describe and explain the matching principle using the adjusting entry for supplies during the month ended May 31, 2008.

8. Which company is more profitable for the month ended May 31, 2008? Would your answer be different if cash basis accounting was used instead of accrual accounting? Explain.

9. Identify the internal controls that Tom's Tots uses to minimize the risk of errors in the accounting system as preventive, detective, or corrective in each of the descriptions below.
   a) The cash balance in the books is compared and reconciled to the bank statement balance.
   b) Tom's Tots requires all discrepancies be investigated and resolved.
   c) One person collects the cash and a different person, who has no access to the cash, records the cash in the accounting records.

Solution

Tom's Tots		Assets =		Liabilities +		Shareholder's equity	
						Contributed capital	Retained earnings
	May 1, 2008 balances	900	Cash	400	Note payable	700 Common stock	600 Retained earnings
		600	Prepaid insurance				
		200	Supplies				
1	Cares for 5 children for a fee of $300 per month for each child; collects cash.	1,500	Cash				1,500 Revenue
2	Pays off the entire loan plus $4 interest	(404)	Cash	(400)	Note payable		(4) Interest expense
3	Pays $500 for May's rent	(500)	Cash				(500) Rent expense
4	Determines that 1/3 of the insurance is used up	(200)	Prepaid insurance				(200) Insurance expense
5	On May 31, only $50 of supplies are lef.	(150)	Supplies				(150) Supplies expense
	May 31, 2008 balances	1,496	Cash			700 Common stock	1,246 Retained earnings
		400	Prepaid insurance				
		50	Supplies				

Tiny Tim's		Assets =	Liabilities +		Shareholder's equity	
					Contributed capital	Retained earnings
	May 1, 2008 balances	900 Cash	400 Note payable		700 Common stock	600 Retained earnings
		600 Prepaid insurance				
		200 Supplies				
1	Cares for 5 children for a fee of $300 per month for each child, to be collected in June	1,500 Accounts receivable				1,500 Revenue
2	Pays $4 interest on the loan	(4) Cash				(4) Interest expense
3	Pays $500 for May's rent	(500) Cash				(500) Rent expense
4	Determines that 1/3 of the insurance is used up	(200) Prepaid insurance				(200) Insurance expense
5	On May 31, only $50 of supplies are left	(150) Supplies				(150) Supplies
	May 31, 2008 balances	396 Cash	400 Note payable		700 Common stock	1,246 Retained earnings
		1,500 Accounts receivable				
		400 Prepaid insurance				
		50 Supplies				

Part B:

<table>
<tr><td colspan="2">

Tom's Tots, Inc.
Income Statement
For the Month Ended May 31, 2008

</td><td colspan="2">

Tiny Tim's, Inc.
Income Statement
For the Month Ended May 31, 2008

</td></tr>
</table>

Tom's Tots, Inc.				Tiny Tim's, Inc.			
Revenue				Revenue			
Service fees earned		$1,500		Service fees earned		$1,500	
Expenses				Expenses			
Rent	$500			Rent	$500		
Supplies	150			Supplies	150		
Insurance	200			Insurance	200		
Interest	4			Interest	4		
Total expenses		854		Total expenses		854	
Net income		$ 646		Net income		$ 646	

Tom's Tots, Inc.
Statement of Changes in Shareholder=s Equity
For the Month Ended May 31, 2008

Tiny Tim's, Inc.
Statement of Changes in Shareholder=s Equity
For the Month Ended May 31, 2008

Tom's Tots, Inc.			Tiny Tim's, Inc.		
Common stock		$ 700	Common stock		$ 700
Beginning retained earnings	$600		Beginning retained earnings	$600	
Plus net income	646		Plus net income	646	
Less distributions to owners	0		Less distributions to owners	0	
Ending retained earnings		1,246	Ending retained earnings		1,246
Total shareholder's equity		$1,946	Total shareholder's equity		$1,946

Tom's Tots, Inc.
Balance Sheet
May 31, 2008

Assets		Liabilities		$ 0
Cash	$1,496	Shareholder=s equity		
Prepaid insurance	400	Common stock	700	
Supplies	50	Retained earning	1,246	
		Total liabilities		
Total assets	$1,946	and equity	$1,946	

Tiny Tim's, Inc.
Balance Sheet
May 31, 2008

Assets		Liabilities		
Cash	$ 396	Note payable	$ 400	
Accounts		Shareholder=s equity		
receivable	1,500	Common stock	700	
Prepaid		Retained earnings	1,246	
insurance	400			
Supplies	50	Total liabilities		
Total assets	$2,346	and equity	$2,346	

Tom's Tots, Inc.
Statement of Cash Flows
For the Month Ended May 31, 2008

Cash from operating activities		
Cash collected from customers	$1,500	
Cash paid for rent	(500)	
Cash paid for interest	(4)	
Total cash from operating activities		$996
Cash from investing activities		0
Cash from financing activities		
Repayment of loan	(400)	
Total cash from financing activities		(400)
Net change in cash		$596

Tiny Tim's, Inc.
Statement of Cash Flows
For the Month Ended May 31, 2008

Cash from operating activities		
Cash paid for rent	$(500)	
Cash paid for interest	(4)	
Total cash from operating activities		$(504)
Cash from investing activities		0
Cash from financing activities		0
Net change in cash		$(504)

Part C **Solution**: Answer the following questions using Parts A and B.

1. Tom's Tots, Inc. and Tiny Tim's, Inc. are both corporations as indicated by the Inc. designation. In addition, the shareholder's equity is separated into common stock and retained earnings. Sole proprietorships and partnerships combine contributed and earned capital into one amount called "capital."

2. Investing in a company as an owner is riskier than as a creditor. There is a legal obligation for a company to pay both interest and principal to its creditors. There is no legal obligation for a company to make any distributions to owners. There is a positive correlation between risk and return, thus an owner should expect a higher return.

3. The separate-entity assumption states that the owner's personal financial records and transactions should not be part of the company's. Only the company's rent expense should be on Tom's Tots' income statement.

4. The monetary-unit assumption requires financial statement items to be measured in monetary units.

5. The historical-cost principle requires Tom's Tots' supplies on hand to be reported at the cost of $50 and not revalued at their current market value of $75.

6. The revenue recognition principle requires revenue to be recorded (recognized) when it is earned (*i.e.*, when goods or services have been delivered) without regard to when the cash is collected from customers. Tiny Tim's reported revenue of $1,500 on the income statement even though no cash has been received from its customers. Accounts receivable of $1,500, an asset on the balance sheet, will show the amount that has not yet been collected from customers. The statement of cash flows will show no cash collected from customers during the period. Thus, the three statements tell three important pieces of information about the sales to customers: 1) the income statement shows the amount of goods or services delivered (revenue); 2) the statement of cash flows shows the amount of cash received; and 3) the balance sheet links the two and shows the amount of revenue not yet collected (accounts receivable).

7. The matching principle requires expenses to be matched on the income statement with the revenue they helped generate. Only the supplies that are used to earn revenue during the period should be expensed. The unused supplies stay on the balance sheet as an asset until they are used.

8. Net income is a measure of profitability. Since both have the same net income. both are equally profitable. If cash basis accounting was used instead of accrual accounting, Tom's Tots would be considered more profitable which is misleading since both companies, in substance, performed equally well. The only difference is that Tiny Tim's did not collect cash from its customers. Accrual accounting better reflects the economic substance of the companies' activities during the month.

9. a) is a detective control; b) is a corrective control; c) is a preventive control.

Review Questions and Exercises

Completion Statements

Fill in the blank(s) to complete each statement.

1. A set of rules called _____ must be followed to help ensure the financial statements are useful.

2. GAAP must be followed when an amount is considered _____, *i.e.*, if it would affect someone=s interpretation or decision.

3. _____ and _____ are needed so that decision-makers can compare the financial statements of one accounting period to other accounting periods and compare one company=s financial statements with other companies=.

4. _____ means the information must be reported in a timely manner and _____ means the information must be accurate and truthful.

5. Before financial statements are prepared, the company must be sure to adjust all account balances to reflect accurate amounts. This process is called _____.

6. A _____ categorizes and lists assets as _____ if the assets will be turned into cash or used up within the year and _____ if the assets will be used for more than one year. It also lists as _____ the liabilities that will be satisfied during the year and _____ if the liabilities will not be satisfied within the year.

7. _____ is the uncertainty associated with the amount and timing of future returns. The higher the _____ the higher the _____.

8. _____ controls such as keeping cash locked up are designed to prevent an error or irregularity.

9. _____ controls such as preparing a cash reconciliation are designed to find an error or irregularity.

10. _____ controls such as denying future credit to slow paying or non-paying customers are designed to fix errors.

True/False

Indicate whether each statement is true (T) or false (F).

_____1. Financial statements prepared using cash basis accounting will never have accounts receivable or accounts payable on the balance sheet.

_____2. Accrual accounting is GAAP; cash basis accounting is not GAAP.

_____3. An owner of a corporation has the legal right to receive interest and dividends.

_____4. Investing as a creditor is riskier than investing as an owner and thus requires a higher return.

_____5. An accrual is recorded when the event occurs before the cash changes hands and a deferral is recorded when the cash changes hands before the event.

_____6. The going-concern assumption assumes a business is going to close in the near future and thus all its assets must be revalued to their current market values.

_____7. An example of a preventive control is to have the same person who has access to cash be the one who maintains the cash records in order to ensure accuracy.

_____8. Company A paid off its $400 note payable, as well as the related interest of $4, on the last day of the accounting period. Company B pays only the interest expense of $4 during the accounting period. As a result, Company A will show a lower net income during this accounting period than it would have had it not paid off the note.

Multiple Choice

Select the best answer for each question.

_____1. Rite-it-up, Inc. purchased land for $20,000 on May 1, 2008. On December 31, 2008, similar land sells for $25,000. The land should be shown on the:
   A. balance sheet as a $25,000 asset.
   B. income statement as revenue of $5,000.
   C. balance sheet as a $20,000 asset.
   D. income statement as an expense of $20,000.

_____2. Ivan Rich is considering lending money to Kneady, Inc. As a potential creditor of Kneady, Inc., Ivan computed Kneady's current ratio in order to measure:
   A. Kneady's ability to replace current assets as they are used.
   B. Kneady's liquidity, i.e., its ability to pay its current debts as they come due.
   C. Kneady's ability to convert its noncurrent assets into current assets.
   D. Kneady's profitability.
   E. The current ratio measures all of the above.

_____3. When an item is immaterial, it means:
   A. it is significant in amount.
   B. it is expressed in dollars instead of some other unit in preparing financial statements.
   C. companies are allowed to ignore recording the small dollar item in the accounting records.
   D. it can be recorded in the most convenient way even if it is not in accordance with GAAP.

_____4. Retained earnings can be found on the:
   A. income statement and statement of cash flows.
   B. statement of changes in shareholders' equity only.
   C. statement of changes in shareholders' equity and the balance sheet.
   D. balance sheet only.

_____5. The owner of Shady Grove Company has the bookkeeper write company checks to pay for his personal items. This violates the:
   A. matching principle.
   B. monetary-unit assumption.
   C. materiality concept.
   D. separate-entity assumption.

_____6. If you were told a company's net income was $100,000, what other information would be helpful in making this more meaningful?
   A. The time period covered.
   B. The method used: accrual or cash basis accounting.
   C. The amount of net income retained versus paid out in dividends.
   D. all of the above

_____7. A company in its first year of business earned revenues of $100,000 but collected only $80,000 in cash from its customers. Which of the following is correct?
   A. The income statement will show revenues of $100,000, the balance sheet will show accounts receivable of $20,000, and the statement of cash flows will show cash collected from customers of $80,000.
   B. The income statement will show revenues of $80,000, the balance sheet will show accounts receivable of $100,000, and the statement of cash flows will show cash collected from customers of $80,000.
   C. The income statement will show revenues of $100,000, the balance sheet will show accounts receivable of $20,000, and the statement of cash flows will show cash collected from customers of $100,000.
   D. The income statement will show revenues of $180,000, the balance sheet will show accounts receivable of $100,000, and the statement of cash flows will show cash collected from customers of $80,000.

_____8. During the year, ABC Company had revenues of $100,000 of which $90,000 has been collected from customers. It also had expenses of $60,000 of which $40,000 has been paid. The owners were paid $20,000 in dividends. Net income for the year equals:
   A. $50,000.
   B. $40,000.
   C. $30,000.
   D. $20,000.

_____9. Which of the following statements about cash is true?
   A. Cash is part of shareholders' equity.
   B. Increases in cash and net income will be the same during an accounting period.
   C. Revenue is earned only when cash is collected.
   D. None of the above is true.

_____10. Which of the following controls is not part of an internal control system?
   A. detective
   B. preventive
   C. liquidity
   D. corrective

Matching

From the list of concepts, principles, and assumptions, write the appropriate letter that best matches each item below. Each term may apply to more than one concept; some may not be used at all.

A.	Accrual accounting	H.	Relevant
B.	Historical-cost principle	I.	Reliable
C.	Consistency	J.	Revenue recognition principle
D.	Comparable	K.	Conservatism
E.	Going-concern assumption	L.	Time-period assumption
F.	Matching principle	M.	Separate-entity assumption
G.	Materiality	N.	Monetary-unit assumption

1.	Which principle is violated when an owner of a company includes his personal expenses in the company's financial records?	
2.	ABC Company records revenues when the goods are delivered even though the cash will not be collected until a later accounting period.	
3.	Inventory is presented in dollars, not units, on the balance sheet.	
4.	Assumes companies are not going to liquidate in the near future and thus helps justify the use of historical cost rather than current cost in valuing assets.	
5.	The accounting information is provided in a timely fashion so that the information is still useful.	
6.	Assets are typically recorded at the amount paid for them.	
7.	Supplies are recorded as an asset and then expensed in the period they are used in helping generate revenue.	
8.	It is important for companies to use the same methods of measuring items on the financial statement each accounting period.	
9.	Comparing financial statements of different companies is more meaningful when the statements are prepared in accordance with GAAP.	
10.	The items on the financial statements should be accurate and truthful.	
11.	Financial statements can be prepared periodically in order to report the progress of the company over its life.	
12.	Accountants should anticipate losses and not gains. They also should not overstate assets.	
13.	Revenues are recorded when earned and expenses are recorded when incurred regardless of when the related cash changes hands.	
14.	Items that are too small to affect anyone's decision making can be recorded in a manner that is not necessarily in accordance with GAAP.	

Exercises

1. Fill in the accounting equation below for Tim's Ware, Inc.'s events that occurred during 2008, its first year of business:

Tim's Ware, Inc.		Assets	=	Liabilities	+	Shareholders' equity	
						Contrib. capital	Retained earnings
a.	Tim's Ware began operations by issuing $6,000 of common stock to its owners.						
b.	Tim's Ware purchased $3,000 of inventory and paid cash.						
c.	Tim's Ware purchased $400 of supplies and paid cash.						
d.	Tim's Ware made sales of $3,300 on account. The cost of the sales was $2,500.						
e.	Tim's Ware collected $2,700 of receivables during the year.						
f.	On July 1, 2008, Tim's Ware paid $2,400 in advance for an insurance policy that covers two years beginning July 1.						
g.	As of December 31, 2008, six months of insurance coverage has expired.						
h.	Supplies on hand as of December 31, 2008 amounted to $100.						

2. Tim's Ware's account titles:		Fill in the correct dollar amount:	Put an "X" in the column of the statement where the item will most likely appear:		
		Amount as of or for the year ended December 31	Income Statement	Balance Sheet	Statement of Cash Flows
a.	Stock issued for cash				
b.	Supplies expense				
c.	Supplies				
d.	Insurance expense				
e.	Prepaid insurance				
f.	Cash paid for insurance				
g.	Cash received from customers				
h.	Accounts receivable				
i.	Sales				
j.	Cost of goods sold				
k.	Inventory				

Solutions to Review Questions and Exercises

Completion Statements

1. GAAP
2. material
3. Consistency; comparability
4. Relevance; reliability
5. adjusting the books
6. Classified balance sheet; current assets; noncurrent assets; current liabilities; noncurrent liabilities
7. Risk; risk; return
8. Preventive
9. Detective
10. Corrective

True/False

1. True   Revenues and expenses are recorded only when cash changes hands under the cash basis accounting, which is not GAAP. Accounts receivable and accounts payable reflect the timing differences between when revenues and expenses are earned and incurred and when the cash later changes hands. These timing differences exist only under accrual accounting, which is required under GAAP.
2. True   See 1. above.
3. False   Creditors have the legal right to receive interest and repayment of principal. Owners have no legal rights to receive dividends.
4. False   See 3. above. In the event of liquidation, creditor obligations must be paid before the owners can receive anything. Since owners are taking more risk, they expect to receive a higher return.
5. True   An example of an accrual is recording an account receivable when revenue is earned before cash is received. An example of a deferral is recording prepaid insurance as an asset when the cash changes hands and later recording the expense when the insurance is used.
6. False   The going-concern assumption assumes companies are not going to liquidate in the near future and thus helps justify valuing assets at their historical cost and not their current market values.
7. False   A preventive control would be to have these duties separated. Those who have access to cash should not do the record keeping. This separation of duties will help ensure that an employee does not pocket cash and then alter the books to conceal the theft.
8. False   The $400 payment of principal reduces assets (cash) and liabilities (notes payable); it does not decrease shareholders' equity. Both will have net income lowered by the same amount, the $4 interest expense.

Multiple Choice

1. C   GAAP require assets to be recorded at historical cost. (You will learn about some exceptions later on in the text.)
2. B   The current ratio is a measure of liquidity and is calculated by dividing current assets by current liabilities.
3. D   Immaterial items can be recorded in a way that does not conform to GAAP as long as it does not have an effect on users' decisions. Immaterial items must be recorded just not in accordance with GAAP.
4. C   The statement of changes in shareholders' equity shows beginning retained earnings plus net income minus dividends to arrive at retained earnings at the end of the accounting period, which also is shown on the balance sheet.

5. D The owner's personal transactions and records must be kept separate from the company's transactions and records.

6. D Financial statements must state the time period covered, which could be a month, quarter or year (A). GAAP require companies to use accrual accounting, which typically results in a better measure of net income than cash basis accounting (which is not GAAP) (B). It is useful to know how much of net income is retained and reinvested into the company versus paid out in dividends to owners; the statement of changes in shareholders' equity shows this amount.

7. A The activity can be summarized as follows:

Assets	Liabilities	Shareholders' equity	
		Contributed capital	Retained earnings
100,000 Accounts receivable (1)			100,000 Revenue (2)
80,000 Cash (3) (80,000) Accounts receivable (4)			

The balance sheet will show ccounts receivable as $20,000 or (1) + (4), the income statement will show revenues as $100,000 (2), and the statement of cash flows will show cash collected from customers as $80,000 (3) in the cash from operating activities section.

8. B Revenues ($100,000) minus expenses ($60,000) equals net income ($40,000). Accrual accounting requires revenues and expenses to be recorded when earned and incurred regardless of when the cash changes hands. In addition, a dividend (which is shown on the statement of changes in shareholders' equity) is not an expense since it does not help generate revenues.

9. D Cash is an asset, not shareholders' equity. Net income and changes in cash are typically different. Net income often includes revenues that may not have been collected and expenses that may not have been paid in the same accounting period as when the revenues were earned and the expenses incurred.

10. C Preventive, detective, and corrective controls are used to minimize the risk of errors in the accounting records.

Matching

1. K Conservatism
2. J Revenue recognition principle
3. L Time-period assumption
4. E Going-concern assumption
5. H Relevant
6. B Historical-cost principle
7. F Matching principle
8. C Consistency
9. D Comparable
10. I Reliable
11. L Time-period assumption
12. K Conservatism
13. A Accrual accounting
14. G Materiality

Exercises

Tim's Ware, Inc.		Assets	Liab.	Shareholders' equity	
				Contrib. capital	Retained earnings
a.	Tim's Ware began operations by issuing $6,000 of common stock to its owners.	6,000 Cash		6,000 Common stock	
b.	Tim's Ware purchased $3,000 of inventory and paid cash.	3,000 Inventory (3,000)Cash			
c.	Tim's Ware purchased $400 of supplies and paid cash.	400 Supplies (400) Cash			
d.	Tim's Ware made sales of $3,300 on account. The cost of the sales was $2,500.	3,300 Accounts receivable (2,500)Inventory			3,300 Sales (2,500) Cost of goods sold
e.	Tim's Ware collected $2,700 of receivables during the year.	2,700 Cash (2,700)Accounts receivable			
f.	On July 1, 2008, Tim's Ware paid $2,400 in advance for an insurance policy that covers two years beginning July 1.	2,400 Prepaid insurance (2,400)Cash			
g.	As of December 31, 2008, six months of insurance coverage has expired.	(600) Prepaid insurance			(600) Insurance expense
h.	Supplies on hand as of December 31, 2008 amounted to $100.	(300) Supplies			(300) Supplies expense

2. Tim's Ware's account titles:		Amount as of or for the year ended December 31	Select one for each line item:		
			Income Statement	Balance Sheet	Statement of Cash Flows
a.	Stock issued for cash	$6,000			X
b.	Supplies expense	$300	X		
c.	Supplies	$100		X	
d.	Insurance expense	$600	X		
e.	Prepaid insurance	$1,800		X	
f.	Cash paid for insurance	$2,400			X
g.	Cash received from customers	$2,700			X
h.	Accounts receivable	$600		X	
i.	Sales	$3,300	X		
j.	Cost of goods sold	$2,500	X		
k.	Inventory	$500		X	

CHAPTER 3
ACCRUALS AND DEFERRALS: TIMING IS EVERYTHING IN ACCOUNTING

Chapter Overview

In Chapter 2, you learned about the difference between cash-basis and accrual-basis accounting. Often there is a difference in timing between a business event and the collection or payment of cash. Chapter 3 deals with accounting for the most common types of business events that involve these timing differences.

Chapter Highlights

1. **Net income** (or **net profit** or **net earnings**) is equal to **revenues** minus **expenses.** The life of a business is continuous, but we must be able to measure income for a shorter period of time, usually a year, quarter, or month. The **income statement**, also called the **statement of operations** or the **profit and loss statement**, reports income earned over a period of time. All revenues earned during the period and all expenses for the period must be included on the income statement. **Timing differences**, the differences between the time when business events take place and the time when cash changes hands, can make it difficult to measure income for a particular accounting period. Companies must make **adjustments** for these timing differences before financial statements can be prepared.

2. **Accruals**, business transactions in which the action takes place before the exchange of cash, can be either revenues or expenses. Making the necessary adjusting entries is called **accruing** revenues or expenses. Accruals affect both the income statement and the balance sheet.

	Revenue	Expenses
Action first	Revenue must be on the income statement even though cash has not yet been collected.	Expenses must be on the income statement even though cash has not yet been paid.

- Interest expense, and the related liability interest payable, must be accrued for all outstanding notes payable. Interest expense is the cost of using someone else's money for a period of time, and it must be shown as an expense on the income statement even though interest has not yet been paid in cash.

Assets	Liabilities	Shareholders' equity	
		Contrib. Cap. +	Retained Earnings
	+Interest payable		- Interest expense

Interest = Principal *times* Rate *times* Time. Keep in mind that interest rates are usually stated as percentages that apply to a full twelve months of borrowing, and be careful to use the correct fraction of a year in calculating interest expense for shorter amounts of time. If cash for this period's accrued interest expense is paid in the following accounting period, the interest expense will not be recorded again. Instead, the payment will reduce both cash and interest payable.

Assets	Liabilities	Shareholders' equity	
		Contrib. Cap. +	Retained Earnings
- Cash	-Interest payable		

- Interest revenue, and the related asset interest receivable, must be accrued on loans the company has made to others. The company has earned interest revenue and must show this revenue on the current period's income statement, even though it has not yet been received in cash.

- At the end of an accounting period, a company must look over its records to make sure that all revenues for services performed or goods delivered to customers are properly recorded. Revenue earned very late in the period may not even have been billed to the customers yet, but it still must be included as revenue on the income statement, and the related accounts receivable must be shown as a current asset on the balance sheet.

Assets	Liabilities	Shareholders' equity	
		Contrib. Cap. +	Retained Earnings
+ AR			+ Sales

When cash is finally collected **(realized)** from these customers in the following accounting period, the company will not record **(recognize)** revenue again. Instead, the company will record an increase in cash and a decrease in accounts receivable.

Assets	Liabilities	Shareholders' equity	
		Contrib. Cap. +	Retained Earnings
+ Cash			
- AR			

- Expenses must be accrued at the end of each accounting period, too. A company must examine all of its business transactions to make sure that no expenses (and related liabilities) have been forgotten because the bills have not yet been received or paid.

- Salary expense is normally recorded when employees are paid. However, the last payday of the accounting period may not be the same as the last day of the accounting period. A company must accrue salary expense for work done by employees between the last payday and the financial statement date. Then the income statement will show the correct salary expense for all work done by employees during the accounting period, and the balance sheet will show the related salaries payable for amounts still owed to employees.

Assets	Liabilities	Shareholders' equity	
		Contrib. Capital +	Retained Earnings
	+ Salaries payable		- Salary expense

On the first payday of the following accounting period, the company must decrease salaries payable for the amount of salary that was reported as a liability in the previous accounting period. It must also decrease retained earnings for any additional salary expense incurred since the beginning of the new accounting period, and decrease cash for the total amount paid to employees.

3. **Deferrals**, business transactions in which the dollars are exchanged before the business activity has occurred, can also be either revenues or expenses.

	Revenue	Expenses
Dollars first	Cash has been received from customers, but the company hasn't done its part to earn it.	Cash has been paid for services or goods not yet used.

- Sometimes a company collects cash from its customers before shipping merchandise to them or performing services for them. The company **defers revenue** when it receives these advance payments. It cannot record revenue yet because it has not done anything to earn the revenue. Instead, the company records the increase in cash, and an increase in **unearned revenue**, a liability.

Assets	Liabilities	Shareholders' equity	
		Contrib. Cap. +	Retained Earnings
+ Cash	+ Unearned revenue		

When the company finally ships the merchandise or performs the service for its customer, it decreases the liability, unearned revenue, and records sales revenue as an increase in retained earnings.

Assets	Liabilities	Shareholders' equity	
		Contrib. Cap. +	Retained Earnings
	- Unearned revenue		+ Sales

- Four kinds of **expenses** are **deferred**, or paid for in advance. A company normally pays for many months of insurance in advance. When insurance coverage is paid for, no insurance expense is recorded. Instead, the company decreases cash and increases **prepaid insurance**, an asset.

Assets	Liab.	Shareholders' equity	
		Contrib. Cap. +	Retained Earnings
+Prepaid insurance - Cash			

When financial statements are prepared, the company makes an adjusting entry to show the expired (used up) part of the insurance coverage as an expense. This adjustment decreases the asset, prepaid insurance, and records insurance expense, which decreases retained earnings.

Assets	Liab.	Shareholders' equity	
		Contrib. Cap. +	Retained Earnings
-Prepaid insurance			-Insurance expense

After this adjusting entry is made, the asset, Prepaid insurance, will show the amount of insurance coverage remaining for future months.

- Like insurance, rent is usually paid in advance. When a company pays cash for rent in advance, it records an increase in an asset, **prepaid rent,** along with a decrease in cash. When financial statements are prepared, an adjusting entry is made to decrease the asset prepaid rent for the amount of rent that has been used up. This adjustment also records rent expense, which decreases retained earnings.

- **Supplies** are miscellaneous items used in a business, and are not the same as **inventory**, which is merchandise purchased for resale. A company will usually buy and pay for supplies in advance. This purchase is recorded as a decrease in cash and an increase in the asset, supplies. As these supplies are used up day by day, no record is made of supplies expense. Instead, at the end of an accounting period, the company counts the supplies that remain. An adjusting entry is made to decrease the asset account, supplies, so that it equals the amount of supplies remaining. The amount of this decrease represents supplies expense, the portion of supplies that have been used up. After this adjusting entry is made, the asset account on the balance sheet properly represents the amount of supplies left for future use. The income statement shows the expense of the supplies that have been used up.

- Often a company will buy an asset like equipment that benefits more than one future accounting period. The whole cost of the equipment is not treated as an expense in the period it is purchased. Instead, the matching principle requires that the cost be spread out over all of the accounting periods that benefit from using the equipment to earn revenue. This is called **depreciating** the asset and the expense reported in each accounting period is known as **depreciation expense**.

When equipment is first purchased, the company decreases cash and increases the asset, equipment.

Assets	Liab.	Shareholders' equity	
		Contrib. Cap. +	Retained Earnings
+Equipment - Cash			

At the end of the accounting period, the company calculates depreciation expense by dividing the cost of the equipment by the number of accounting periods it will be used. The adjusting entry records depreciation expense, which decreases retained earnings, and **accumulated depreciation**, a **contra-asset**.

Assets	Liab.	Shareholders' equity	
		Contrib. Cap. +	Retained Earnings
-Accumulated depreciation			-Depreciation expense

Accumulated depreciation is considered an asset account, but it is subtracted from equipment in the calculation of total assets on the balance sheet. The company's balance sheet will continue to show the cost of the equipment, but along with this cost the company will report accumulated depreciation, the total depreciation that has been recorded for the equipment so far. Cost minus accumulated depreciation is the **book value** or **carrying value** of the equipment.

4. **Working capital** is equal to **current assets** minus **current liabilities**. It measures a company's ability to finance operations. The **quick ratio,** also called the **acid-test ratio**, is another measure of a company's ability to pay its short-term liabilities. It adds together a company's three most liquid assets: cash, short-term investments, and net accounts receivable; and divides them by total current liabilities.

5. There are three significant risks associated with financial records and accounting information. The first risk is errors in recording and updating the accounting records. Input and processing controls are designed to make sure that only authorized transactions are entered in the accounting records. Reconciliation and control reports are designed to catch errors in the input and processing of accounting data. Computerized accounting systems can make sure that the accounting equation is in balance at every stage of data entry. Documentation can provide support for recorded transactions.

The second major risk is unauthorized access to accounting information, which exposes a company to leaks of confidential information and makes it possible for perpetrators to cover up theft by altering the accounting records. Accounting records should be kept in a secure location. Computerized systems have user IDs and passwords that limit access to the system. Firms should also carefully screen employees.

The third major risk is loss or destruction of accounting data. Computerized systems need to store backup data at a remote location.

Featured Exercise

For each question below, fill in the correct dollar amount and circle the correct financial statement on which it appears, using the following code:

    IS for the income statement for the year ended December 31, 2010
    BS for the balance sheet at December 31, 2010
    SOCF for the statement of cash flows for the year ended December 31, 2010

1. On September 1, 2010, Acme Enterprises borrowed $10,000 from the bank on a two-year, 9% note payable. All interest will be paid when the loan is repaid. On December 31, 2010, the correct adjusting entry was made for interest.

    a. Cash received from borrowing of $_____ appears on the: **IS**   **BS**   **SOCF**

    b. Interest payable of $_____ appears on the: **IS**   **BS**   **SOCF**

    c. Notes payable of $_____ appears on the: **IS**   **BS**   **SOCF**

    d. Interest expense of $_____ appears on the: **IS**   **BS**   **SOCF**

    e. Cash paid for interest of $_____ appears on the: **IS**   **BS**   **SOCF**

2. On October 1, 2010, Acme Enterprises loaned $100,000 to its CEO on a one-year, 12% note receivable. All interest will be received when the loan is collected. On December 31, 2010, the correct adjusting entry was made for interest.

    a. Notes receivable of $_____ appears on the: **IS   BS   SOCF**

    b. Interest receivable of $_____ appears on the: **IS   BS   SOCF**

    c. Interest revenue of $_____ appears on the: **IS   BS   SOCF**

    d. Cash received for interest of $_____ appears on the: **IS   BS   SOCF**

3. On December 30, 2010, Acme Enterprises completed a $2,000 consulting job for a client. Because most of the company employees are celebrating the New Year a little early, no one billed the customer when the job was finished. However, on December 31, 2010, the correct adjusting entry was made.

    a. Cash received from customers of $_____ appears on the: **IS   BS   SOCF**

    b. Accounts receivable of $_____ appears on the: **IS   BS   SOCF**

    c. Revenue of $_____ appears on the: **IS   BS   SOCF**

4. Acme Enterprises pays its employees every other Friday. The last payday was Friday, December 23, 2010, and the next payday will be Friday, January 6, 2011. Employees earned $3,500 in the last week of December, 2010. The correct adjusting entry was made on December 31.

    a. $_____ of this $3,500 appears as cash paid to employees on the: **IS   BS   SOCF**

    b. $_____ of this $3,500 appears as salary expense on the: **IS   BS   SOCF**

    c. Salaries payable of $_____ appears on the: **IS   BS   SOCF**

5. On August 1, 2010, Acme Enterprises received $6,000 in advance from a customer for services that Acme expected to perform over the next twelve months. The entire $6,000 was properly recorded as unearned revenue. On December 31, 2010, the correct adjusting entry was made.

    a. Revenue of $_____ appears on the: **IS   BS   SOCF**

    b. Unearned revenue of $_____ appears on the: **IS   BS   SOCF**

    c. Cash received from customers of $_____ appears on the: **IS   BS   SOCF**

6. On April 1, 2010, Acme Enterprises paid $1,200 for a 24-month insurance policy that went into effect the same day. On December 31, 2010, the correct adjusting entry was made.

    a. Cash paid for insurance of $_____ appears on the: **IS   BS   SOCF**

    b. Prepaid insurance of $_____ appears on the: **IS   BS   SOCF**

    c. Insurance expense of $_____ appears on the: **IS   BS   SOCF**

7. On January 1, 2010, Acme Enterprises had $1,000 of supplies in its supply room. During 2010, Acme paid $5,000 cash for more supplies. On December 31, 2010, Acme counted the supplies and found that only $800 of supplies remained. On December 31, 2010, the correct adjusting entry was made.

   a. Supplies of $_____ appears on the: **IS**   **BS**   **SOCF**

   b. Supplies expense of $_____ appears on the: **IS**   **BS**   **SOCF**

   c. Cash paid for supplies of $_____ appears on the: **IS**   **BS**   **SOCF**

8. On January 1, 2010, Acme Enterprises bought a delivery truck for $30,000 cash. The company expects to use the truck for six years. On December 31, 2010, the correct adjusting entry was made.

   a. Equipment of $_____ appears on the: **IS**   **BS**   **SOCF**

   b. Depreciation expense of $_____ appears on the: **IS**   **BS**   **SOCF**

   c. Cash paid for depreciation of $_____ appears on the: **IS**   **BS**   **SOCF**

   d. Accumulated depreciation of $_____ appears on the: **IS**   **BS**   **SOCF**

   e. Cash paid for equipment of $_____ appears on the: **IS**   **BS**   **SOCF**

Solution

1. a. Cash received from borrowing of **$10,000** appears on the **SOCF**.
   b. Interest payable of **$300** appears on the **BS**.
   c. Notes payable of **$10,000** appears on the **BS**.
   d. Interest expense of **$300** appears on the **IS**.
   e. Cash paid for interest of **$0** appears on the **SOCF**.

2. a. Notes receivable of **$100,000** appears on the **BS**.
   b. Interest receivable of **$3,000** appears on the **BS**.
   c. Interest revenue of **$3,000** appears on the **IS**.
   d. Cash received for interest of **$0** appears on the **SOCF**.

3. a. Cash received from customers of **$0** appears on the **SOCF**.
   b. Accounts receivable of **$2,000** appears on the **BS**.
   c. Revenue of **$2,000** appears on the **IS**.

4. a. **$0** of this $3,500 appears as cash paid to employees on the **SOCF**.
   b. **$3,500** of this $3,500 appears as salary expense on the **IS**.
   c. Salaries payable of **$3,500** appears on the **BS**.

5. a. Revenue of **$2,500** appears on the **IS**.
   b. Unearned revenue of **$3,500** appears on the **BS**.
   c. Cash received from customers of **$6,000** appears on the **SOCF**.

6. a. Cash paid for insurance of **$1,200** appears on the **SOCF**.
   b. Prepaid insurance of **$750** appears on the **BS**.
   c. Insurance expense of **$450** appears on the **IS**.

7. a. Supplies of **$800** appear on the **BS**.
   b. Supplies expense of **$5,200** appears on the **IS**.
   c. Cash paid for supplies of **$5,000** appears on the **SOCF**.

8. a. Equipment of **$30,000** appears on the **BS**.
   b. Depreciation expense of **$5,000** appears on the **IS**.
   c. Cash paid for depreciation of **$0** appears on the **SOCF**.
   d. Accumulated depreciation of **$5,000** appears on the **BS**,
   e. Cash paid for equipment of **$30,000** appears on the **SOCF**.

Review Questions and Exercises

Completion Statements

Fill in the blank(s) to complete each statement.

1. Working capital is _____ minus _____.

2. The book value of equipment is _____ minus _____.

3. An asset that is subtracted from other assets to calculate total assets is called a _____.

4. The _____ principle requires that the cost of equipment be treated as an expense over all of the accounting periods the equipment is used.

5. Two financial statements, the _____ and the _____ are affected by adjusting entries.

6. Interest equals _____ times _____ times _____.

7. When a company receives payment in advance, it records _____, a liability.

8. Before financial statements can be prepared, _____ entries must be recorded for accruals.

True/False

Indicate whether each statement is true (T) or false (F).

_____ 1. The income statement is also known as a profit and loss statement.

_____ 2. Interest expense is recorded only after it is paid in cash.

_____ 3. Accruals involve business events that take place before cash is received or paid.

_____ 4. Supplies are part of a company's inventory.

_____ 5. Interest receivable must be accrued on notes payable.

_____ 6. Deferrals involve cash collected or paid before a business event takes place.

_____ 7. The cost of equipment is an expense of the period when it is purchased.

_____ 8. Most companies pay for insurance coverage in advance.

_____ 9. Controls can eliminate all business risks.

_____ 10. Depreciation expense is always the same amount as accumulated depreciation.

Multiple Choice

Select the best answer for each question.

_____ 1. The adjusting entry to record an accrued expense also involves recording a(n):
A. revenue.
B. asset.
C. liability.
D. decrease in cash.

_____ 2. The adjusting entry to record an accrued revenue also involves recording a(n):
A. expense.
B. asset.
C. liability.
D. increase in cash.

_____ 3. When a company pays for six months insurance in advance, it records:
A. prepaid insurance, an asset.
B. insurance expense, a liability.
C. prepaid insurance, an expense.
D. insurance expense, a decrease in retained earnings.

_____ 4. When a company receives cash in advance for services it has not yet performed, it records:
A. revenue earned.
B. unearned service revenue, a liability.
C. unearned service revenue, an asset.
D. This is a trick question. Nothing is recorded until services are performed.

_____ 5. ABC, Inc., shows $300 of Supplies expense on its income statement. ABC must have:
A. purchased $300 of supplies during the period.
B. paid cash for $300 of supplies during the period.
C. used $300 of supplies during the period.
D. The answer cannot be determined from the information given.

6. During June, Busy Beaver bought $5,000 of office supplies on account, and promised to pay the vendor the full amount in July. At the end of June, Busy Beaver estimated that there were $2,000 of office supplies left unused. How much supplies expense should Busy Beaver report for June?
   A. $5,000
   B. $2,000
   C. $3,000
   D. $ 0

7. During June, Busy Beaver performed $3,500 of services for clients on account. In June, $500 of this amount was collected in cash. The remaining $3,000 was collected in July. How much service revenue should Busy Beaver report for June?
   A. $ 0
   B. $500
   C. $3,000
   D. $3,500

8. Salaries payable on a company's balance sheet indicates that:
   A. the company is in serious financial difficulty. It does not even have enough cash to pay its employees.
   B. the company's accountants are seriously confused. Salaries appear on the income statement, not the balance sheet.
   C. employees had not received payment for the last few days of work because the last day of the accounting period was not a payday.
   D. employees were overpaid and now owe the company money.

9. Accounts receivable appear on a company's balance sheet because the company:
   A. collected cash when it sold merchandise to customers.
   B. sold merchandise to customers but has not received payment yet.
   C. bought merchandise on account.
   D. paid for merchandise previously purchased on account.

10. The accountant for Ace Electronics forgot to make the adjusting entry for depreciation on the company's equipment. As a result of this mistake:
    A. net income is too high.
    B. total liabilities are too low.
    C. net income is too low.
    D. stockholders' equity is too low.

Matching

Adjusting entries affect both the income statement and the balance sheet. The left-hand column below lists revenue and expense accounts commonly used in adjusting entries. Match each of these income statement accounts with a related balance sheet account that would appear in an adjusting entry with the revenue or expense.

Income statement		**Balance sheet**	
_____	1. Subscription revenue	A.	Accumulated depreciation
_____	2. Interest revenue	B.	Supplies
_____	3. Interest expense	C.	Prepaid rent
_____	4. Depreciation expense	D.	Interest payable
_____	5. Supplies expense	E.	Salaries payable
_____	6. Insurance expense	F.	Interest receivable
_____	7. Salary expense	G.	Prepaid insurance
_____	8. Rent expense	H.	Unearned revenue

Exercises

Show the effect on the accounting equation of each of the events described. This company has a fiscal year that ends on December 31.

1		Assets =	Liabilities +	Owners' Equity
a	On December 31, made an adjusting entry to accrue $3,000 of sales revenue earned that has not yet been billed to a customer			
b	On January 2, billed the customer for $3,000			
c	On January 15, collected all $3,000 in cash			

2		Assets =	Liabilities +	Owners' Equity
a	On October 31, paid $2,400 for six months' rent in advance			
b	Made the adjusting entry required on December 3.			

46

3		Assets =	Liabilities +	Owners' Equity
a	On June 1, borrowed $10,000 for two years at 9% interest; interest will be paid when the loan is repaid.			
b	Made the adjusting entry required on December 31			

4		Assets =	Liabilities +	Owners' Equity
a	On August 1, loaned $20,000 for two years at 12% interest; interest will be collected when the loan is repaid.			
b	Made the adjusting entry required on December 31			

5		Assets =	Liabilities +	Owners' Equity
a	On December 30, the last working day of the year, employees have earned $1,800. They will not be paid for another week. Make the adjusting entry required on December 31.			
b	Paid employees $4,000 for work done in December and January			

6		Assets =	Liabilities +	Owners' Equity
a	Noticed that only $100 of office supplies remain in the back room; bought $700 more office supplies on account.			
b	Paid the vendor for the office supplies purchased in (6a) above			
c	On December 31, $200 of office supplies are left in the back room; made the adjusting entry required on December 31			

7		Assets =	Liabilities +	Owners' Equity
a	On June 21, paid $9,000 for rent for the six months beginning August 1			
b	Made the adjusting entry required on December 31			
c	On December 21, paid $10,000 for rent for the six months beginning February 1 of next year			
d	Made the adjusting entry required on December 31			

8		Assets =	Liabilities +	Owners' Equity
a	On December 28, received a $75 bill for electric service used between November 25 and December 25.; Ppayment is not due until January 10.			
b	On January 10, paid December's $75 electric bill			
c	On December 31, the company still had not received the December bill from the gas company. This bill usually runs about $225 for winter months.			
d	December's gas bill for $230 arrived on January 3. The bill was paid on January 15.			

9		Assets =	Liabilities +	Owners' Equity
a	On January 1, bought a $3,600 copy machine, which is expected to last for three years			
b	Made the adjusting entry required on December 31			

Solutions to Review Questions and Exercises

Completion Statements

1. current assets, current liabilities
2. cost, accumulated depreciation
3. contra-asset
4. matching
5. income statement, balance sheet
6. principal, rate, time
7. unearned revenue
8. adjusting

True/False

1. True
2. False: Interest expense must be accrued for notes payable.
3. True
4. False: Supplies are miscellaneous items used in a business. Inventory is merchandise purchased for resale.
5. False: Interest expense and interest **payable** must be accrued on notes payable.
6. True
7. False: The matching principle requires that the cost of equipment be treated as an expense over all of the accounting periods when the equipment is used, not just the period when it is purchased.
8. True
9. False

10. False: Depreciation expense is just the current period's depreciation. Accumulated depreciation is all of the depreciation expense that has ever been recorded for a particular asset. In the first accounting period an asset is used, accumulated depreciation will be the same as Depreciation expense. In later accounting periods, accumulated depreciation will be more than Depreciation expense for the period.

Multiple Choice

1. C   Expenses are accrued because something has been used up to earn revenue, but cash has not been paid yet. The liability to make future payment for something already used up must be recorded as well.

2. B   Revenues are accrued because they have been earned and should appear on the income statement. However, cash has not yet been received in exchange for goods or services already delivered. The right to receive cash in the future from this revenue is an asset.

3. A   In exchange for payment for six months of future insurance coverage, the company gets an asset, prepaid insurance, because the company will receive future benefit from the insurance policy. Adjusting entries are needed to turn the asset into an expense as the coverage is used up.

4. B   The company has not done anything yet to earn the advance payment it has received. The company should record a liability because it owes its customer services now that it has accepted payment in advance.

5. C   Supplies are an expense when they are used to earn revenue. Purchasing supplies creates an asset called supplies, which the company has on hand to use in the future. Payment for supplies removes a liability to pay for items already received.

6. C   Supplies become an expense when they are used in the business to earn revenue. This company started with $5,000 of supplies, but has only $2,000 left unused. The missing $3,000 of supplies must have been used up, and should be reported as an expense.

7. D   Revenue is recorded when it is earned by performing services for clients. It does not matter when cash is collected.

8. C   The last payday of the accounting period rarely is the same as the date of the financial statements. However, the income statement must show as an expense all that employees earned for the period. Any amounts that have not been paid in cash yet are shown as salaries payable, a liability on the balance sheet. Almost every company will routinely show salaries payable because of timing differences. So it does not mean a company is unable to pay its employees. (However, if salaries payable are very large when compared with salary expense for the year, it might mean the company has some financial problems.)

9. B   Accounts receivable are created when a company earns revenue and has the right to receive cash from customers.

10. A   The missing entry would record depreciation expense and accumulated depreciation. Depreciation expense, like all expenses, decreases net income, retained earnings, and total stockholders' equity. Without the missing expense, net income, retained earnings, and total stockholders' equity are all too high, not too low. Accumulated depreciation is a contra-asset that decreases total assets. Neither depreciation expense nor accumulated depreciation has any effect on liabilities.

Matching

H 1. Subscription revenue/ Unearned revenue
F 2. Interest revenue/ Interest receivable
D 3. Interest expense/ Interest payable
A 4. Depreciation expense/ Accumulated depreciation
B 5. Supplies expense/ Supplies

G 6. Insurance expense/ Prepaid insurance
E 7. Salary expense/ Salaries payable
C 8. Rent expense/ Prepaid rent

Exercises

1		Assets =	Liabilities +	Owners' Equity
a	On December 31, made an adjusting entry to accrue $3,000 of sales revenue earned that has not yet been billed to a customer *The income statement must show all revenue earned during the year.*	$3,000 Accounts receivable		$3,000 Sales
b	On January 2, billed the customer for $3,000 *No entry is required because revenue has already been recorded in the previous accounting period.*	No entry	No entry	No entry
c	On January 15, collected all $3,000 in cash *Revenue is recorded in December, when it is earned, not when cash is collected.*	3,000 Cash (3,000) Accounts receivable		

2		Assets =	Liabilities +	Owners' Equity
a	On October 31, paid $2,400 for six months' rent in advance *This prepayment is an asset because it will provide future benefit. No expense will be recorded until the rent is used up.*	(2,400) Cash 2,400 Prepaid rent		
b	Made the adjusting entry required on December 31 *Two months of rent have been used up.* *$2,400/6 x 2 months = $800*	(800) Prepaid rent		(800) Rent expense

3		Assets =	Liabilities +	Owners' Equity
a	On June 1, borrowed $10,000 for two years at 9% interest; interest will be paid when the loan is repaid. *No interest expense is recorded until the company has used the $10,000 for a period of time.*	10,000 Cash	10,000 Notes payable	
b	Made the adjusting entry required on December 31 *The company has used the borrowed cash for seven months.* *$10,000 x .09 x 7/12 = $525*		525 Interest payable	(525) Interest expense

4		Assets =	Liabilities +	Owners' Equity
a	On August 1, loaned $20,000 for two years at 12% interest; interest will be collected when the loan is repaid. *Interest is earned as time goes by. However, on the date of the loan, no time has elapsed so no interest is recorded yet.*	20,000 Notes receivable (20,000) Cash		
b	Made the adjusting entry required on December 31 *The loan has earned interest for 5 months. $20,000 x .12 x 5/12 = $1,000*	1,000 Interest receivable		1,000 Interest revenue

5		Assets =	Liabilities +	Owners' Equity
a	On December 30, the last working day of the year, employees have earned $1,800. They will not be paid for another week. Make the adjusting entry required on December 31. *Expenses are recorded when they are used to earn revenue.*		1,800 Salaries payable	(1,800) Salary expense
b	Paid employees $4,000 for work done in December and January *$1,800 of the cash has already been recorded as an expense in December. $4,000 – 1,800 = $2,200*	(4,000) Cash	(1,800) Salaries payable	(2,200) Salary expense

6		Assets =	Liabilities +	Owners' Equity
a	Noticed that only $100 of office supplies are left in the back room; bought $700 more office supplies on account *The supplies will be used in the future, so they are recorded as an asset.*	700 Supplies	700 Other payables	
b	Paid the vendor for the office supplies purchased in (6a) above *No expense is recorded when cash is paid for a liability.*	(700) Cash	(700) Other payables	
c	On December 31, $200 of office supplies are left in the back room; made the adjusting entry required on December 31 *Supplies used are an expense. $100 + 700 – 200 = $600*	(600) Supplies		(600) Supplies expense

7		Assets =	Liabilities +	Owners' Equity
a	On June 21, paid $9,000 for rent for the six months beginning August 1 *This rent will be used in the future, so it is recorded as an asset.*	9,000 Prepaid rent (9,000) Cash		
b	Made the adjusting entry required on December 31 *Five month's rent has been used up.* *$9,000/6 months x 5 months = $7,500*	(7,500) Prepaid rent		(7,500) Rent expense
c	On December 21, paid $10,000 for rent for the six months beginning February 1 of next year	10,000 Prepaid rent (10,000) Cash		
d	Made the adjusting entry required on December 31 *No entry is required because none of the rent prepaid on December 21 has expired yet.*	no entry	no entry	no entry

8		Assets =	Liabilities +	Owners' Equity
a	On December 28, received a $75 bill for electric service used between Nov. 25 and December 25; payment is not due until January 10. *The electricity was used to earn revenue in December, so it should be an expense in December even though it has not been paid in cash.*		75 Other payables	(75) Utilities expense
b	On January 10, paid December's $75 electric bill *The $75 was already recorded as an expense in December. Expenses are not recorded when liabilities are paid.*	(75) Cash	(75) Other payables	
c	On December 31, the company still had not received the December bill from the gas company. This bill usually runs about $225 for winter months. *The company must estimate and record the expense so December's utility expense will be included on the income statement.*		225 Other payables	(225) Utilities expense
d	December's gas bill for $230 arrived on January 3. The bill was paid on January 15. *Most of the December bill was accrued as an expense in December, and should not be expensed in January, too. The December estimate was $5 too low, so January's income statement will include $5 extra expense. Estimates are never perfect, but this $5 is immaterial.*	(230) Cash	225 Other payables	(5) Utilities expense

9		Assets =	Liabilities +	Owners' Equity
a	On January 1, bought a $3,600 copy machine, which is expected to last for three years *The equipment is an asset because it will benefit future accounting periods.*	3,600 Equipment (3,600) Cash		
b	Made the adjusting entry required on December 31 *The cost of the equipment must be spread out over all the years it will be used.* *$3,600 / 3 years = $1,200*	(1,200) Accumulated depreciation		(1,200) Depreciation expense

CHAPTER 4
ACQUISITION AND USE OF LONG-TERM OPERATIONAL ASSETS

Chapter Overview

A business acquires **long-term operational** (or **fixed**) **assets** such as property, plant, and equipment that will be used in the business. From Chapter 4, you should understand how to account for the purchase, use, and sale of these long-term assets.

Chapter Highlights

1. There are two types of long-term assets. **Tangible assets** are assets used in the business to help generate revenue. They can be seen and touched and include property, plant, equipment, and natural resources. **Intangible assets**, whose true value resides in the rights and privileges given to their owners, include copyrights, patents, franchises, trademarks, and goodwill.

2. When a long-term asset is purchased, its cost is **capitalized**, meaning the cost is recorded as an asset rather than an expense. Since the asset is used to generate revenue, the matching principle requires the cost of the asset to be allocated to an expense on the income statement over the periods it is used. This process of **expensing (writing off)** the cost of a long-term asset to expense is called **depreciation** for plant and equipment, **depletion** for natural resources, and **amortization** for intangible assets. Land is the only long-term asset that remains on the books at cost.

3. The **historical cost principle** requires that a long-term asset be recorded at its purchase price plus any costs necessary to get the asset in place and ready to use. Such additional costs may include freight-in, transportation insurance, installation costs, commissions, architect and attorney fees, construction costs, and the costs of renovating, repairing, or preparing the asset for use.

4. Two or more long-term assets are sometimes bought for a single price. These assets may depreciate at different rates or not at all (land). Thus, the assets must be recorded separately.

The **relative fair market value method** is used to assign the joint costs to the individual assets using the individual assets' market values or appraisal values at the time of purchase. The fair market value of a single asset is divided by the sum of the assets' fair market values to arrive at a percentage. This percentage is then multiplied by the total cost to get an asset's individual cost.

5. **Capitalizing** a cost means to record the cost as an asset on the balance sheet. Any expenditure that will benefit more than one accounting period is called a **capital expenditure**. As the asset is used to help generate revenue, it will become an expense on the income statement. **Depreciation** is a systematic, rational allocation of the cost of a fixed asset to expense over the periods benefited and does not measure the actual physical deterioration or decrease in market value of the asset. The **book value** (or **carrying value**) of an asset is the cost of the asset minus **accumulated depreciation** (all the depreciation taken to date).

6. GAAP allows three common methods of depreciation for financial statements.

- **Straight-line depreciation** is a simple method in which depreciation expense is the same amount each accounting period. Depreciation expense equals the depreciable base divided by the estimated useful life of the asset. The **depreciable base** equals the cost of the asset minus its salvage value. The **salvage value** (or residual value) is what the company estimates it can sell the asset for when it is done using it. The **estimated useful life** is the number of periods the company estimates it will benefit from the use of the asset.

- **Activity depreciation,** also called **units - of - production depreciation,** calculates the depreciation rate by dividing the depreciable base by the estimated total units of activity the asset will provide. This depreciation rate is then multiplied by the actual number of units used or produced during an accounting period. The activity and straight-line methods differ in that the activity method 1) uses units (not time) in the denominator, 2) requires multiplying the number of actual units used or produced during the accounting period by the depreciation rate, and 3) may result in different depreciation expense each period depending on the amount of use.

- **Declining balance depreciation method** is an **accelerated method** that allows for more depreciation expense in the early years and less in the later years of an asset's life. A common rate used is 200% and is called **double-declining balance** because the rate at which an asset is depreciated is 200% or twice that of the straight-line rate. For example, if the life of an asset is 5 years, the straight-line rate is 1/5 or 20% and the double-declining balance rate is twice that, or 2/5 or 40%. Depreciation expense for the period is calculated by multiplying the asset's book value (*not its cost*) by the double-declining balance rate. Since the book value is cost minus accumulated depreciation, the book value will become smaller every period the asset is depreciated. Thus, each later period's depreciation expense is smaller than the prior period's expense. Since salvage value is not built into the double-declining balance calculation, the depreciation will need to be adjusted to ensure the net book value equals the salvage value by the end of its useful life.

7. The effect of the adjusting entry to record depreciation (or use of an asset) during an accounting period is the same regardless of the method used:

Assets	Lia.	Shareholders' equity	
		CC	**Retained earnings**
- Accumulated depreciation			- Depreciation expense

The income statement will show depreciation expense for the accounting period. Depreciation expense will be closed into retained earnings at the end of each accounting period. Accumulated depreciation, unlike depreciation expense, accumulates, so its balance equals all the depreciation taken to date, not just the current period's depreciation.

The balance sheet will show:
Cost
Minus accumulated depreciation
Net book value

The net book value is the amount of undepreciated historical cost

8. **Depletion** is the systematic write-off of the cost of natural resources, *e.g.* forests, oil, and mineral deposits. It is similar to the activity depreciation method. A depletion rate is found by dividing the cost of the natural resource, minus its salvage value, by the estimated total units to be produced over its life. The units of the natural resource produced are board feet of lumber, barrels of oil, tons of ore, etc. The depletion rate per unit is then multiplied by the actual number of units produced in a given accounting period.

9. **Amortization** of intangible assets such as copyrights, patents, franchises, etc., is similar to straight-line depreciation. An intangible asset is amortized over the shorter of its useful life or legal life. If an intangible asset has an indefinite useful life, it is not amortized, but the firm will periodically evaluate it for any permanent decline in value and write it down if necessary.

Goodwill results from one company purchasing another company at a price that is greater than the market value of net assets. The purchased assets are recorded at their market values, and goodwill is recorded as an intangible asset. Goodwill is not amortized, but must be evaluated regularly and written down if it has declined in value.

Research and development (R&D) costs must be expensed immediately (*i.e.*, not capitalized) since it is too uncertain that the costs will result in future benefit. Software development costs are considered R&D expenses until they result in a product that is technologically feasible, after which additional costs from that time on must be capitalized.

10. Every time it prepares financial statements, a company must review its long-term assets for **impairment**, the permanent reduction of market value below book value.

11. A **revenue expenditure** has no future benefit beyond the current accounting period, and is an expense on the income statement. The matching principle requires **expensing** the cost in the same period as the related revenue, hence the term revenue expenditure. Companies usually have policies that dictate whether a cost is a capital expenditure (an asset) or revenue expenditure (an expense).

- For the sake of efficiency, the materiality principle allows companies to expense certain small-dollar capital expenditures rather than capitalizing them and later having to depreciate them over time. An example would be the purchase of a $10 wastebasket.

- Costs to repair or remodel a long-term asset are capital expenditures if they increase the useful life, efficiency, or productivity of the asset. These costs are added to the historical cost of the asset, and future depreciation expense is revised based on the new book value of the improved asset, its salvage value, and its remaining useful life.

- Ordinary repairs are revenue expenditures because they are routine and do not significantly increase the life or efficiency of an asset. Painting, re-shingling a roof, and tune-ups for vehicles and machines are examples of revenue expenditures.

12. The asset's useful life and salvage value are estimates made by managers that may later need to be revised because of additional information. Revising an estimate is not treated as an error; it does not require restating previous records and financial statements. The revision is used only for future periods by adjusting the depreciation formula using the net book value (cost minus accumulated depreciation) and the new residual value or useful life.

- For example, an asset cost $1,000, had a salvage value of $100 and a useful life of 3 years. Its net book value at the end of the first year using straight-line is $700. At the end of the second year, management decided to revise the residual value to $200 and the useful life to 4 more years. The depreciation will now be changed to equal the net book value ($700) minus the new residual value ($200) depreciated over the new estimated useful life of 4 years.

13. When a company finally sells an asset at the end of its useful life, the price often differs from the net book value. The result is a gain if the amount received is greater than the net book value or a loss if the amount received is less than the net book value. Both the asset and its accumulated depreciation must be removed from the company's books.

- A machine that originally cost $1,000 with accumulated depreciation of $800 at the end of its useful life has a net book value equal to its estimated residual value of $200. If the **proceeds** (or price the asset sells for) are $300, then a gain is recorded:

Assets	Lia.	Sh. equity	
		CC	**Retained earnings**
$ 300 Cash (1,000) Machine 800 Accumulated depreciation			$200 Gain on sale of machine

If the machine sold for only $150, then a loss would be recorded:

Assets	Lia.	Sh. equity	
		CC	**Retained earnings**
$ 150 Cash (1,000) Machine 800 Accumulated depreciation			$(50) Loss on sale of machine

- Gains or losses from sales of assets not sold in the ordinary course of business are reported on the income statement, usually below the subtotal "operating income."

14. The financial statements provide useful information for decision-makers regarding long-term assets. The balance sheet reports the cost, the accumulated depreciation (depletion or amortization), and the net book value of long-term assets that reflects the future usefulness of the assets. The income statement includes depreciation (depletion and amortization) expense (not necessarily as separate line items). The expense reflects the use of the asset during the current accounting period matched with the related revenue the asset helped to generate. Finally, the notes to the financial statements provide additional useful information such as the depreciation methods used and the useful lives of the long-term assets. The investing activities section of the statement of cash flows shows cash paid for long term-assets and cash received from selling long-term assets.

15. A ratio that measures how well a company is using its assets to generate revenue is **return on assets** (or ROA) and equals net income plus interest expense, divided by average total assets. Since ROA is a measure of how well owners' (not creditors') money is used, interest expense (which is the creditors' return on their money) is added back to net income in the numerator. ROA is meaningful only when compared to ROA from other years or other companies.

16. Another ratio that evaluates a firm's use of assets is the **asset turnover ratio:** net sales divided by average total assets. This ratio varies significantly from one industry to another, so it is important to compare only firms in the same industry.

17. Safeguarding assets is one of the main purposes of an internal control system in minimizing the risk of theft or damage. Physical controls that limit access to assets are important and can be as simple as locks on doors. Complete and reliable record keeping is also an important control. **Segregation of duties** is vital, so those responsible for record keeping are different from those who have physical custody of the assets. The assets and related records and controls should be monitored on an on-going basis, often by a company's own internal auditors. Intangible assets pose special risks. The rise of technology and the Internet has created major concerns about copyright violations.

18. (Appendix) GAAP are the rules followed in preparing financial statements. The Internal Revenue Code dictates the legal rules used for preparing federal tax returns. A significant difference in the rules is the method of depreciating assets. A common method on tax returns that is not allowed on GAAP financial statements is the **Modified Accelerated Cost Recovery System (MACRS)**. This method results in assets being written off very quickly. The high deduction for depreciation results in lower taxable income and lower federal income taxes. Lower taxes (which must be paid in cash) should increase a company's cash flow for the year, giving it more cash to invest in the purchase of additional assets, which in turn will help it to earn additional revenue.

Featured Exercise

On January 1, 2009, the San Diego Sea World purchased Arco the whale from the Washington Coast Aquarium. Arco cost $500,000 plus 5% sales tax. The transportation costs included $4,000 for an 11-ton truck and crane, $100,000 for airfare, and $1,000 transportation insurance premiums. The San Diego Sea World paid $50,000 in fish food, $6,000 annual insurance premiums, and $20,000 in training and maintenance costs for Arco during 2009. Arco's estimated useful life is 10 years and 8,000 performances. The residual value for Arco is 5,000 pounds at $2 per pound. Arco performed in 750 shows during 2009 and 820 during 2010.

Required:

Part A: Identify which costs the San Diego Sea World should capitalize (*i.e.*, capital expenditures) and which costs should be expensed (*i.e.*, revenue expenditures) for the year ended December 31, 2009.

Part B: What is the effect of depreciation on San Diego Sea World's accounting equation?

Assets	Liabilities	Shareholders' equity	
		CC	**Retained earnings**

Part C: Calculate the depreciation expense, accumulated depreciation and the net book value of Arco the whale using the three depreciation methods (straight-line, activity, and double-declining balance methods) for the years ended December 31, 2009 and 2010.

Straight-line method	Depreciation expense	Accumulated depreciation	Net book value
Year ended December 31, 2009			
Year ended December 31, 2010			

Activity method	Depreciation expense	Accumulated depreciation	Net book value
Year ended December 31, 2009			
Year ended December 31, 2010			

Double-declining balance method	Depreciation expense	Accumulated depreciation	Net book value
Year ended December 31, 2009			
Year ended December 31, 2010			

Part D: Show the effect of the sale of Arco for $14,000 at the end of his useful life assuming a net book value of $10,000 at the time of sale.

Assets	Liabilities	Shareholders' equity	
		CC	Retained earnings

Solution

Part A: The costs to get Arco in place and ready to perform that should be capitalized:

Whale	$500,000
Sales tax (0.05 x $500,000)	25,000
Truck and crane rental	4,000
Airfare	100,000
Transportation insurance	1,000
Total cost of whale	$630,000

The costs that are revenue expenditures are as follows:

Fish food	$ 50,000
Insurance premiums	6,000
Training and maintenance	20,000
Depreciation	(amount depends on method used)

Part B:

Assets	Liabilities	Shareholders' equity	
		CC	Retained earnings
-Accumulated depreciation			-Depreciation expense

Part C:

Straight-line method:

Year ended	Depreciation expense	Accumulated depreciation	Net book value
December 31, 2009	$62,000	$(62,000)	$568,000
December 31, 2010	$62,000	$(124,000)	$506,000

Depreciation expense on the income statement for the year ended December 31, 2009 is $62,000.

$$\frac{\text{Cost - residual value}}{\text{Estimated useful life}} = \frac{\$630,000 - (\$2 \times 5,000 \text{ pounds})}{10 \text{ years}} = \$62,000$$

Accumulated depreciation on the balance sheet at December 31, 2009 is $(62,000)

The net book value of Arco on the balance sheet at December 31, 2009 is $568,000 or the cost minus accumulated depreciation ($630,000 - 62,000).

Depreciation expense on the income statement for the year ended December 31, 2010 is $62,000.

$$\frac{\text{Cost - residual value}}{\text{Estimated useful life}} = \$62,000 \text{ (same for each year)}$$

Accumulated depreciation (a contra asset) on the balance sheet at December 31, 2010 is $(124,000) or $(62,000) for each of the two years combined.

The net book value of Arco on the balance sheet at December 31, 2010 is $506,000 or the cost minus accumulated depreciation ($630,000 - 124,000).

Activity method:

Year ended	Depreciation expense	Accumulated depreciation	Net book value
December 31, 2009	$58,125	$(58,125)	$571,875
December 31, 2010	$63,550	$(121,675)	$508,325

Depreciation expense on the income statement for the year ended December 31, 2009 is $58,125.

$$\text{Depreciation rate} = \frac{\text{Cost - residual value}}{\text{Estimated total performances}} = \frac{\$630,000 - 10,000}{8,000} = \$77.50 \text{ per performance}$$

Depreciation expense = Depreciation rate x performances in 2009 = $77.50 x 750 = $58,125.

Accumulated depreciation on the balance sheet at December 31, 2009 is $(58,125).

The net book value of Arco on the balance sheet at December 31, 2009 is $571,875 or the cost minus accumulated depreciation ($630,000 - 58,125).

Depreciation expense on the income statement for the year ended December 31, 2010 is $63,550.

Depreciation rate x performances in 2010 = $77.50 x 820 = $63,550.

Accumulated depreciation on the balance sheet at December 31, 2010 is $(121,675) or

$(58,125) beginning accumulated depreciation plus $(63,550) accumulated depreciation for 2010.

The net book value of Arco on the balance sheet at December 31, 2010 is $508,325 or the cost minus accumulated depreciation (or $630,000 - 121,675).

Double-declining balance method:

Year ended	Depreciation expense	Accumulated depreciation	Net book value
December 31, 2009	$126,000	$(126,000)	$504,000
December 31, 2010	$100,800	$(226,800)	$403,200

Depreciation expense on the income statement for the year ended December 31, 2009 is $126,000.

$$\text{Net book value} \times \frac{2}{\text{Estimated useful life}} = (\$630,000 - 0) \times \frac{2}{10} = \$126,000.$$

Accumulated depreciation on the balance sheet at December 31, 2009 is $(126,000).

The net book value of Arco on the balance sheet at December 31, 2009 is $504,000 or the cost minus accumulated depreciation ($630,000 - 126,000).

Depreciation expense on the income statement for the year ended December 31, 2010 is $100,800.

$$\text{Net book value} \times \frac{2}{\text{Estimated useful life}} = (\$630,000 - 126,000) \times \frac{2}{10} = \$100,800.$$

Accumulated depreciation on the balance sheet at December 31, 2010 is $(226,800) or $(126,000) beginning accumulated depreciation plus (100,800) accumulated depreciation for 2010.

The net book value of Arco on the balance sheet at December 31, 2010 is $403,200 or the cost minus accumulated depreciation (or $630,000 - 226,800).

Part D: Proceeds minus net book value = $14,000 - 10,000 = $4,000 gain on sale of Arco.

Assets	Liabilities	CC	Shareholders' equity
			Retained earnings
$14,000 Cash (630,000) Whale 620,000 Accumulated depreciation			$4,000 Gain on sale of whale

Review Questions and Exercises

Completion Statements

Fill in the blank(s) to complete each sentence.

1. _____ can be seen and touched and include property, plant, equipment, and natural resources.

2. _____ whose true value resides in the rights and privileges given to the owners, include copyrights, patents, franchises, trademarks, and goodwill.

3. When a long-term asset is purchased, its cost is _____ or is recorded as an asset rather than an expense.

4. The _____ is a common method used to assign the joint costs to the individual assets using the individual assets' market values, or appraisal values, at the time of purchase.

5. The cost of an asset minus its accumulated depreciation is called _____.

6. The depreciation expense using the straight-line method equals _____.

7. The depreciation expense using the activity method equals _____.

8. _____ is an_____ that allows for more depreciation expense in the early years and less in the later years of an asset's life.

9. A _____ benefits only the current accounting period. It is an expense on the income statement.

10. The formula for calculating asset turnover is _____.

True/False

Indicate whether each statement is true (T) or false (F).

1. Capital expenditures are costs that are found on the balance sheet as assets; revenue expenditures are costs that are found on the income statement as expenses.

2. Depreciation expense will always be higher in the first year of an asset's life when the double-declining balance method is used instead of the straight-line method.

3. A gain on the sale of a long-term asset will result when the salvage value is greater than the proceeds.

4. A basket purchase allocation is required when the items purchased are all revenue expenditures and the costs are less than their relative fair market values.

5. Despite the method of depreciation chosen by a company, the amount of accumulated depreciation will be the same at the end of the asset's useful life.

6. Despite the method of depreciation chosen by a company, the amount of depreciation expense will be the same each accounting period.

7. Despite the method of depreciation chosen by a company, the effect on the accounting equation is to decrease assets and decrease owners' equity.

8. The return on assets will increase if a company purchases inventory on account instead of paying cash.

9. Internal controls surrounding the safeguarding of assets include monitoring the assets by comparing the physical assets to what is recorded in the information system.

10. (Appendix) MACRS is a depreciation method used only for financial reporting, not tax reporting.

Multiple Choice

Select the best answer for each question.

_____1. Which of the following should be recorded as an intangible asset?
    A. research and development costs on a new project
    B. cost of advertising a new product
    C. cost of employee education
    D. cost to obtain exclusive rights to manufacture a unique product

_____2. Which financial statement shows how much cash was paid for newly acquired property plant and equipment?
    A. statement of financial position
    B. statement of operations
    C. statement of cash flows
    D. statement of changes in shareholders' equity

_____3. Which of the following accounting treatments violates the matching principle?
    A. A capital expenditure is recorded as an asset when acquired and expensed as it generates revenue.
    B. A revenue expenditure is recorded as an expense.
    C. A long-term asset is expensed over its useful life using one of the depreciation methods in accordance with GAAP.
    D. None of the above violates the matching principle.

_____4. The bookkeeper did not record depreciation expense for the period. As a result:
    A. assets will be understated.
    B. liabilities will be understated.
    C. owners' equity will be overstated
    D. There is no effect on the accounting equation because accumulated depreciation is a contra asset account that offsets depreciation expense.

_____5. The bookkeeper recorded a capital expenditure as an asset. As a result:
    A. assets will be understated.
    B. liabilities will be understated.
    C. owners' equity will be overstated
    D. There is no effect on the accounting equation because capital expenditures should be recorded as assets, not expenses.

_____6. The net book value (or carrying value) of an asset is
    A. increased when the market value of the asset increases.
    B. the original cost of the asset minus its salvage value minus its accumulated depreciation.
    C. the amount for which the asset could be sold.
    D. the original cost of the asset minus its accumulated depreciation.

_____7. E-buy, Inc. purchased a mainframe computer for $500,000 with state sales tax of $20,000. It cost $1,000 to transport, $5,000 to install and $10,000 to test the computer. Six months later, the computer was cleaned for $500 and a programmer was paid $300 to make adjustments to the programs that back up the accounting information system. The proper treatment in recording these events is to:

A. capitalize $500,000 as an asset on the balance sheet and show $36,800 as expenses on the income statement.
B. capitalize $520,000 as an expense on the balance sheet and $16,800 as revenue expenditures on the balance sheet.
C. capitalize $536,000 as an asset on the balance sheet and show $800 as expenses on the income statement.
D. capitalize $536,800 as an asset on the balance sheet.

_____8. The process of expensing the cost of an intangible asset over its useful life is called:
A. amortization.
B. depreciation.
C. depletion.
D. accumulated depreciation.
E. None of the above is correct. An intangible asset is not expensed over its useful life.

_____9. The process of expensing the cost of a natural resource over its useful life is called:
A. amortization.
B. depreciation.
C. depletion.
D. accumulated depreciation.
E. None of the above is correct. Natural resources are not expensed over their useful lives.

_____10. Fair Market, Inc. purchased land, a warehouse and a delivery truck for $450,000. The appraised values for the items are $300,000, $150,000, and $50,000, respectively. Fair Market should record this purchase:
A. as an expense of $450,000 on the income statement.
B. as assets on the balance sheet: $270,000 for the land, $135,000 for the building, and $45,000 for the delivery truck.
C. as assets on the balance sheet: $300,000 for the land, $150,000 for the building, and $50,000 for the delivery truck.
D. as assets on the balance sheet: $500,000 for basket purchase minus $50,000 accumulated depreciation.

Exercises

For Exercises 1 - 4: Fill in the correct dollar amount and put an "X" in the column of the financial statement where the item will most likely be found.

1. On April 1, 2009, AAA, Inc. paid $36,000 cash for a truck. AAA plans to use the truck for 5 years and then sell it for $6,000. The straight-line depreciation method was used. Give the adjusting journal entry required at the end of April and at the end of May.

Financial statement line item:	Amount as of or for the month ended April 30	Income Statement	Balance Sheet	Statement of Cash Flows
a. Cash paid for truck				
b. Depreciation expense				
c. Accumulated depreciation				
d. Truck (net of accumulated depreciation)				

Financial statement line item:	Amount as of or for the month ended May 31	Income Statement	Balance Sheet	Statement of Cash Flows
e. Cash paid for truck				
f. Depreciation expense				
g. Accumulated depreciation				
h. Truck (net of accumulated depreciation)				
i. Cash paid for depreciation expense				

2. On January 1, 2010, E-commerce began operations and purchased a truck for $25,000 cash. This truck has an estimated useful life of 4 years and a salvage value of $5,000. The straight-line depreciation method was used.

Financial statement line item:	Amount as of or for the year ended December 31, 2010	Select one for each line item:		
		Income Statement	Balance Sheet	Statement of Cash Flows
a. Depreciation expense				
b. Accumulated depreciation				
c. Truck (net of accumulated depreciation)				

Financial statement line item:	Amount as of or for the year ended December 31, 2011	Select one for each line item:		
		Income Statement	Balance Sheet	Statement of Cash Flows
d. Depreciation expense				
e. Accumulated depreciation				
f. Truck (net of accumulated depreciation)				

On January 1, 2012, E-commerce sold the truck (in 2. above) for $12,000.

Financial statement line item:	Amount as of or for the year ended December 31, 2012	Select one for each line item:		
		Income Statement	Balance Sheet	Statement of Cash Flows
g. Gain (loss) on sale of truck				
h. Proceeds from sale of truck				

66

3. On January 1, 2009, Slippery Slope, Inc. purchased equipment for $400,000 cash. This equipment has an estimated useful life of 10 years and a salvage value of $20,000. The **double-declining depreciation method** was used.

Financial statement line item:	Amount as of or for the year ended December 31, 2009	Select one for each line item:		
		Income Statement	Balance Sheet	Statement of Cash Flows
a. Depreciation expense				
b. Accumulated depreciation				
c. Equipment (net of accumulated depreciation)				

Financial statement line item:	Amount as of or for the year ended December 31, 2010	Select one for each line item:		
		Income Statement	Balance Sheet	Statement of Cash Flows
d. Depreciation expense				
e. Accumulated depreciation				
f. Equipment (net of accumulated depreciation)				

4. On January 1, 2010, Tons-of-Coal, Inc. purchased mining equipment for $70,000, which had an estimated useful life of five years or 200,000 tons of coal and an estimated residual value of $10,000. Tons-of-Coal used the activity method of depletion and the machine produced 35,000 tons in 2010 and 40,000 in 2011.

Financial statement line item:	Amount as of or for the year ended December 31, 2010	Select one for each line item:		
		Income Statement	Balance Sheet	Statement of Cash Flows
a. Depreciation expense				
b. Accumulated depreciation				
c. Machinery (net of accumulated depreciation)				

Financial statement line item:	Amount as of or for the year ended December 31, 2011	Select one for each line item:		
		Income Statement	Balance Sheet	Statement of Cash Flows
d. Depreciation expense				
e. Accumulated depreciation				
f. Machinery (net of accumulated depreciation)				

5. a. Show the effect on the accounting equation for each of the following:

	Assets	Lia.	Shareholders' equity	
			CC	Retained earnings
a. On January 1, 2011, Ridof, Inc. sold its van for $1,000 cash. The van had cost $20,000 and had $18,000 in accumulated depreciation. Record the sale of the van.				
b. Changes, Inc. revised its truck's estimated useful life from 5 years to 4 years at the beginning of its 3rd year. Record depreciation for year 3 given that the truck cost $60,000, had accumulated depreciation of $20,000, a residual value of $10,000 and uses the straight-line method.				

c. Safety, Inc. paid $200 for a special insurance policy to cover the delivery of a new machine.				
d. Fixit, Inc. paid $100 to pay for routine repairs of its copy machine.				
e. Expand, Inc. built a $50,000 addition to its building by borrowing from the bank.				
f. Expand, Inc. paid $500 in architect fees related to the addition to its building in e., above.				
g. Tops, Inc. paid $3,000 for a newly shingled roof.				
h. Accume, Inc. recorded $1,000 amortization on its copyright.				
i. Accume, Inc. recorded $3,000 depreciation on its fixed assets.				
j. Rand, Inc. spent $800,000 on research and development during the year.				

6. Calculate the 2010 return on assets and asset turnover ratio for Rachio, Inc. given the selected information from its financial statements:

As of or for the year ended	December 31, 2010	December 31, 2009
Current assets	$18,000	$20,000
Long-term assets	$27,000	$35,000
Current liabilities	$10,000	$10,000
Long-term liabilities	$15,000	$15,000
Sales	$100,000	$90,000
Net income	$4,000	$5,000

Solutions to Review Questions and Exercises

Completion Statements

1. Tangible assets
2. Intangible assets
3. capitalized
4. relative fair market value method
5. net book value (or carrying value)
6. (Cost – salvage value) / estimated useful life
7. ((Cost – salvage value) / estimated total units) times the units produced or used during the period.
8. Declining-balance method, accelerated method
9. Revenue expenditure
10. Net sales divided by average total assets

True/False

1. True
2. True
3. False   A gain on the sale of a long-term asset will result when the net book value is less than the proceeds.
4. False   A basket purchase allocation is needed when the items are purchased together for a single price. The costs must be separated and can be allocated based on their relative fair market values.
5. True
6. False   Depreciation expense may differ depending on the method of depreciation used. Straight-line will result in the same expense each accounting period; depreciation expense using the activity method will vary depending on the level of activity; and depreciation expense using the declining-balance method will be higher in the early periods compared to the later years of the life of the asset.
7. True
8. False   The return on assets will decrease if a company purchases inventory on account because the denominator will increase while the numerator would be the same as if cash had been paid instead.
9. True
10. False   MACRS is a depreciation method used only for tax reporting. The accelerated method used for financial reporting is the declining balance method.

Multiple Choice

1. D   Research and development costs, employee education and training costs, and advertising are all revenue expenditures that are expensed, not capitalized.
2. C   The cash flow from investing activities section of the statement of cash flows shows how much cash was spent on purchases of long-term assets. The balance sheet shows the balances of long-term assets, their related accumulated depreciation (depletion or amortization), and their net book value. The income statement shows the depreciation (depletion or amortization) expense for the period.
3. D   The matching principle requires costs to be expensed in the period the items help generate revenue. Capital expenditures and long-term assets are not expensed because they will help to

generate revenues in the future. Revenue expenditures are expensed in the current period since they benefit the current period.

4. C The adjusting entry to record depreciation (depletion and amortization) is to reduce assets and reduce shareholders' equity. Shareholders' equity and the assets were not properly reduced, so they will be overstated.

5. D A capital expenditure should be recorded as an asset since it will provide future benefit.

6. D The net book value of an asset is found on the balance sheet and represents the undepreciated balance (or cost minus accumulated depreciation).

7. C All costs incurred to get an asset in place and ready to use are capitalized. Once the asset is in place and being used, the costs for ordinary repairs and upkeep are expensed (revenue expenditures).

8. A The process of expensing the cost of an intangible asset is amortization, the cost of expensing a fixed asset (except land) is depreciation, and the cost of expensing natural resources is depletion.

9. C The process of expensing the cost of an intangible asset is amortization, the cost of expensing a fixed asset (except land) is depreciation, and the cost of expensing natural resources is depletion.

10. B The relative fair market value method allocates the cost as follows:
Land: ($300,000/($300,000 + $150,000 + $50,000)) x $450,000 = $270,000
Warehouse: ($150,000/($300,000 + $150,000 + $50,000)) x $450,000 = $135,000
Truck: ($50,000/($300,000 + $150,000 + $50,000)) x $450,000 = $45,000.

Exercises

1. Financial statement line item:	Amount as of or for the month ended April 30	Select one for each line item:		
		Income Statement	Balance Sheet	Statement of Cash Flows
a. Cash paid for truck	$36,000			X
b. Depreciation expense	$36,000 - 6,000 / 60 months	X		
c. Accumulated depreciation	$500		X	
d. Truck (net of accumulated depreciation)	$36,000 - 500 = $35,500		X	

1. Financial statement line item:	Amount as of or for the month ended May 31	Select one for each line item: (if applicable)		
		Income Statement	Balance Sheet	Statement of Cash Flows
e. Cash paid for truck	$0			Not shown
f. Depreciation expense	$36,000 - 6,000 / 60 months	X		
g. Accumulated depreciation	$1,000		X	
h. Truck (net of accumulated depreciation)	$36,000 - 1,000 = $35,000		X	
i. Cash paid for depreciation expense	$0			Not shown

71

2. Financial statement line item:	Amount as of or for the year ended December 31, 2010	Income Statement	Balance Sheet	Statement of Cash Flows
a. Depreciation expense	$\dfrac{\$25,0000 - 5,000}{4 \text{ years}}$	X		
b. Accumulated depreciation	$5,000		X	
c. Truck (net of accumulated depreciation)	$25,000 - 5,000 = $20,000		X	

2. Financial statement line item:	Amount as of or for the year ended December 31, 2011	Income Statement	Balance Sheet	Statement of Cash Flows
d. Depreciation expense	$\dfrac{\$25,000 - 5,000}{4 \text{ years}}$	X		
e. Accumulated depreciation	$5,000 + 5,0000 = $10,000		X	
f. Truck (net of accumulated depreciation)	$25,000 - 10,000 = $15,000		X	

2. Financial statement line item:	Amount as of or for the year ended December 31, 2012	Income Statement	Balance Sheet	Statement of Cash Flows
g. Gain (loss) on sale of truck	$12,000 - 15,000 = ($3,000)	X		
h. Proceeds from sale of truck	$12,000			X

3. Financial statement line item:	Amount as of or for the year ended December 31, 2009	Income Statement	Balance Sheet	Statement of Cash Flows
a. Depreciation expense	$400,000 x 2/10 = $80,000	X		
b. Accumulated depreciation	$80,000		X	
c. Equipment (net of accumulated depreciation)	$400,000 - 80,000 = $320,000		X	

3. Financial statement line item:	Amount as of or for the year ended December 31, 2010	Income Statement	Balance Sheet	Statement of Cash Flows
d. Depreciation expense	$320,000 x 2/10 = $64,000	X		
e. Accumulated depreciation	$80,000 + 64,000 = $144,000		X	
f. Equipment (net of accumulated depreciation)	$400,000 - 144,000 = $256,000		X	

4. Financial statement line item:	Amount as of or for the year ended December 31, 2010	Select one for each line item:		
		Income Statement	Balance Sheet	Statement of Cash Flows
a. Depreciation expense	(($70,000 - 10,000)/200,000 tons) x 35,000 tons = $10,500	X		
b. Accumulated depreciation	$10,500		X	
c. Machinery (net of accumulated depreciation)	$70,000 - 10,500 = $59,500		X	

4. (continued) Financial statement line item:	Amount as of or for the year ended December 31, 2011	Select one for each line item:		
		Income Statement	Balance Sheet	Statement of Cash Flows
d. Depreciation expense	(($70,000 - 10,000)/200,000 tons) x 40,000 tons = $12,000	X		
e. Accumulated depreciation	$10,500 + 12,000 = $22,500		X	
f. Machinery (net of accumulated depreciation)	$70,000 - 22,500 = $47,500		X	

5.	Assets	Lia.	Shareholders' equity	
			CC	Retained earnings
a.	$1,000 (20,000) 18,000			$(1,000)
b.	(15,000) or $60,000 - 20,000 - 10,000 = $15,000 / 2 years			(15,000)
c.	200 (200)			
d.	(100)			(100)
e.	50,000	50,000		
f.	500 (500)			
g.	(3,000)			(3,000)
h.	(1,000)			(1,000)
i.	(3,000)			(3,000)
j.	(800,000)			(800,000)

6. ROA = Net income/Total average assets = $5,000/(($55,000 + 45,000)/2) = 0.1 or 10%
   Asset turnover ratio = Net sales/Total average assets = $100,000/(($55,000 + 45,000)/2) = 2.0

CHAPTER 5
THE PURCHASE AND SALE OF INVENTORY

Chapter Overview

Chapter 5 focuses on the operating cycle for a merchandising company: starting with cash, the company buys inventory, sells the inventory, and collects cash from customers. In this chapter you will learn how a company accounts for the purchase and sale of inventory and how this information is reported in the financial statements.

Chapter Highlights

1. The acquisition process is well controlled when a company requires the use of the following documents and procedures:

- A **purchase requisition**, a document requesting goods or services needed by someone in the company, should be sent to the company's purchasing agent who obtains the required authorizations and determines the best place to obtain the goods or services.

- The purchasing agent specifies what is needed in a **purchase order,** which is then sent to the selected vendor, the receiving department, and the accounts payable department.

- The receiving department will let the accounts payable department know when the goods have arrived. Accounts payable will pay for the goods when it has a vendor invoice to match with the purchase order.

2. When a company uses a **perpetual inventory system**, every purchase of inventory is recorded as an increase in the inventory account. Each time an item is sold, the company moves the cost of the inventory sold from the inventory account to cost of goods sold. Therefore, at any given point in time, the balance in the inventory account represents the **cost of goods available for sale.**

3. If the terms of purchase are **FOB shipping point**, then the buyer pays the shipping cost. Freight paid by the purchasing company is called **freight-in** and is included in the buyer's inventory cost. If the terms are **FOB destination**, then the seller pays the shipping cost. Delivery expense for the seller is called **freight-out** and is an operating expense on the seller's income statement.

4. **Purchase returns** reflect the amount of goods the purchasing company returned to the vendor. **Purchase allowances** are price reductions the vendor allowed for defective goods kept by the company. Purchase returns and allowances decrease the cost of inventory.

5. **Purchase discounts**, offered by vendors for prompt payment, also reduce the cost of inventory. Discounts are expressed in terms such as 2/10, n/30, which means that the buyer gets a 2% discount if the bill is paid within 10 days. Otherwise, no discount will be given and the full amount of the bill is due within 30 days. Buyers should always take cash discounts, since missing the discount adds 2% to their cost, but gives them only a 20-day extension in time to pay. This amounts to a 36% annual interest rate in a 360-day year.

If a company purchases $300 of inventory on account, terms 1/10, n/30, the $300 is recorded as an increase in both inventory and accounts payable. If the purchasing company takes the 1% cash discount, it reduces the amount of cash the company pays and the value of its inventory:

Assets	Liabilities	Sh. Equity	
		CC	RE
300 Inventory	300 AP		
(297) Cash (3) Inventory	(300) AP		

6. Sales revenue is recognized either when the goods are shipped (FOB shipping point) or when they arrive at the buyer's place of business (FOB destination). **Sales returns and allowances** and **sales discounts** are **contra-revenue** accounts

74

that are subtracted from sales on the income statement to calculate **net sales**.

7. Most retail firms must collect a percentage of sales as sales tax for the state government. Sales tax increases the amount of cash or accounts receivable, but not the amount of sales revenue. Instead, sales taxes payable is recorded as a current liability.

8. Some companies still use a **periodic inventory system** rather than a perpetual system. With a periodic system, cost of goods sold can be calculated only after a physical count of inventory is taken. The inventory account does not show a running balance of the cost of goods available for sale, but is updated only at the end of the accounting period. With advances in technology, many companies are now able to use a perpetual inventory system instead, which has the advantage of providing current information about inventory and cost of goods sold at all times. It also allows a company to identify inventory shrinkage by comparing its perpetual records with a physical count of inventory.

9. In calculating cost of goods sold on the income statement, companies do not have to track the actual cost of each specific inventory item sold. This would be too time-consuming and expensive for companies that make many purchases at continually changing costs. GAAP allows companies to select one of several inventory cost flow assumptions when determining the cost of goods sold. The method used does not have to be consistent with the actual physical flow of goods. Since the various methods can result in significantly different amounts, GAAP requires companies to disclose the amounts and methods used in the notes to the financial statements. The four basic methods used to calculate cost of goods sold and the cost of ending inventory are:

- **Specific identification method**. The cost of goods sold equals the actual cost of the specific goods that have been sold. This method is the only method where the cost flow is consistent with the physical flow of goods. Companies that purchase a small quantity of easily-identifiable, luxury items typically use this method.

- **Weighted-average method**. An average unit cost is calculated by dividing the total cost of goods available for sale by the total number of units available for sale. The average unit cost is then multiplied 1) by the number of units sold to arrive at cost of goods sold on the income statement and 2) by the number of units remaining unsold to arrive at ending inventory on the balance sheet.

- **First-in, first-out method (FIFO)**. Regardless of which specific items are sold, FIFO assumes the first goods purchased are the first goods sold. Cost of goods sold is the cost of the older items available for sale and ending inventory is the cost of the most recent purchases.

- **Last-in, first-out method (LIFO)**. Regardless of which specific items are sold, LIFO assumes the most recently purchased goods are sold first. Cost of goods sold is the cost of the newer items available for sale and ending inventory is the cost of the older items.

10. A company has to decide not only which inventory cost flow method to use, but also when to record its cost of goods sold. A company will use one of two options:

- A **perpetual inventory** system records cost of goods sold and updates the inventory account after every sale. Two entries are required: one to record the sale and the other to record the cost of the sales. For example:

Assets	Lia.	Shareholders' Eq.	
		CC	**RE**
60 AR or Cash			60 Sales
(25) Inventory			(25) COGS

With a perpetual system, careful attention must be paid to the dates of purchases and sales.

- A **periodic inventory** system records cost of goods sold and updates the inventory balance only after a physical count of inventory at the end of each accounting period. When a sale is made only one entry is recorded:

Assets	Lia.	Shareholders' Eq.	
		CC	RE
60 AR or Cash			60 Sales

After a physical inventory count at the end of the accounting period, cost of goods sold and ending inventory are determined, using weighted-average, FIFO, or LIFO.

11. The choice of inventory method affects the amounts shown for cost of goods sold on the income statement and inventory on the balance sheet. A company might choose a method used by other companies in the same industry, in order to make its financial statements comparable; or it might choose the method that results in lower income taxes and higher cash flows.

When prices are rising, LIFO, which uses the newer, higher prices as cost of goods sold, will report a higher cost of goods sold, lower income, and lower ending inventory. Lower reported income means lower income taxes and higher cash from operating activities because less cash is used to pay taxes. Since the IRS requires that companies using LIFO for tax purposes must also use LIFO for financial reporting, many companies choose to use LIFO.

On the other hand, a manager whose bonus is tied to reported profits might choose to use FIFO, which uses lower, older prices as cost of goods sold. Lower cost of goods sold means higher reported net income and a higher bonus for the manager.

12. GAAP requires inventory to be valued on the balance sheet using the **lower-of-cost-or-market (LCM) rule**, to help prevent inventory from being overstated. Market value is the inventory's replacement cost, which is the cost to buy similar inventory. If the market value is lower than the historical cost of inventory, then the value of the inventory must be reduced. Firms that deal in cutting-edge technology are most likely to have inventory that becomes obsolete.

13. A company's **gross profit ratio** shows the percentage of sales dollars a company has left after covering its cost of goods sold. It should be large enough to cover a company's other operating expenses and have something left over for profit.

$$\text{Gross profit ratio} = \frac{\text{Gross profit}}{\text{Sales}}$$

Retailers are particularly concerned with their gross profit ratios. Companies that sell a high volume of merchandise generally have lower gross profit ratios than companies with low sales volumes.

The **inventory turnover ratio** shows how quickly a company is selling and replacing its inventory.

$$\text{Inventory turnover ratio} = \frac{\text{Cost of goods sold}}{\text{Average inventory}}$$

The inventory turnover ratio varies significantly from one industry to another. Managers can calculate the number of days' sales in inventory by dividing 365 days by the inventory turnover ratio.

14. There are significant risks associated with inventory that can be reduced by good internal control policies and procedures. In addition to controls such as selecting a reliable vendor and making sure that the items received are the ones that were ordered, companies should limit access to inventory by using locked storage rooms. Segregation of duties means that those who keep the inventory records should not have physical access to inventory.

15. (Appendix 5A) An error in ending inventory will affect both cost of goods sold and net income.

Beginning inventory
+Purchases
Goods available for sale
-Ending inventory
Cost of goods sold

If ending inventory is too high, too much is subtracted from goods available for sale and cost of goods sold will be too low This makes net income on the income statement too high. If, on the other hand, ending inventory is too low, then too little is subtracted from goods available for sale and cost of goods sold will be too high. This makes net income on the income statement too low.

If the error is not discovered before the next year's financial statements are prepared, then this year's incorrect ending inventory becomes next year's incorrect beginning inventory. If this year's ending inventory is too high, then next year's beginning inventory will also be too high. Both cost of goods available for sale and cost of goods sold will be too high next year. Net income will be understated. On the other hand, if this year's ending inventory is too low, then next year's beginning inventory will also be too low. Both cost of goods available for sale and cost of goods sold will be too low next year. Net income will be overstated.

Total income for the two years combined will be correct, but it is important that each year's income statement be correct as well.

16. (Appendix 5B) The **gross profit method** allows companies to estimate inventory rather than actually counting it. A company may use this method to estimate inventory for monthly or quarterly financial statements or to estimate lost inventory for insurance claims. Estimated inventory is calculated by first calculating the company's typical gross profit percentage (gross profit divided by sales) from prior periods. Second, the company multiplies the sales for the period by the estimated gross profit percentage to arrive at an estimated gross profit margin. Third, the sales minus the estimated gross profit margin equals the estimated cost of goods sold. Fourth, the ending inventory can then be determined by subtracting the estimated cost of goods sold from the goods available for sale (beginning inventory plus purchases).

Featured Exercise

The Ultimate Snowboard Shop's records showed the following information about its beginning inventory, purchases, and sales of snowboards for January:

	Units	Unit Price
Beginning inventory, January 1	10	$200
Purchase, January 15	10	$210
Purchase, January 18	20	$220
Sale, January 20	36	$450
Purchase, January 23	10	$230

Part A: For each question below, fill in the correct dollar amount and circle the correct financial statement on which it appears, using the following code:

> **IS** for the income statement for the month ended January 31
> **BS** for the balance sheet at January 31
> **SOCF** for the statement of cash flows for the month ended January 31

1. Assume Ultimate uses a **LIFO perpetual** inventory system.

    a. Cost of goods sold of $_____ appears on the: **IS   BS   SOCF**

    b. Inventory of $_____ appears on the: **IS   BS   SOCF**

    c. Sales of $_____ appears on the: **IS   BS   SOCF**

    d. Gross margin of $_____ appears on the   **IS   BS   SOCF**

2. Assume Ultimate uses a **LIFO periodic** inventory system.

    a. Cost of goods sold of $_____ appears on the: **IS   BS   SOCF**

    b. Inventory of $_____ appears on the: **IS   BS   SOCF**

    c. Sales of $_____ appears on the: **IS   BS   SOCF**

    d. Gross margin of $_____ appears on the   **IS   BS   SOCF**

3. Assume Ultimate uses a **FIFO perpetual** inventory system.

    a. Cost of goods sold of $_____ appears on the: **IS   BS   SOCF**

    b. Inventory of $_____ appears on the: **IS   BS   SOCF**

    c. Gross margin of $_____ appears on the   **IS   BS   SOCF**

4. Assume Ultimate uses a **FIFO periodic** inventory system.

    a. Cost of goods sold of $_____ appears on the: **IS**   **BS**   **SOCF**

    b. Inventory of $_____ appears on the: **IS**   **BS**   **SOCF**

    c. Gross margin of $_____ appears on the   **IS**   **BS**   **SOCF**

5. Assume Ultimate uses a **weighted average periodic** inventory system.

    a. Cost of goods sold of $_____ appears on the: **IS**   **BS**   **SOCF**

    b. Inventory of $_____ appears on the: **IS**   **BS**   **SOCF**

    c. Gross margin of $_____ appears on the: **IS**   **BS**   **SOCF**

6. Which method, LIFO, FIFO, or Weighted-average method, is the right answer for the following questions?

    a. Which method results in the highest net income?

    b. Which method results in the lowest taxes?

    c. Which method results in the highest inventory turnover rate?

    d. Which method results in the highest current ratio?

    e. Which method results in the highest gross margin on sales percentage?

Solution

Part A:

    1. LIFO perpetual:
    a. (20 x $220) + (10 x $210) + (6 x $200) = $7,700; IS
    b. (4 x $200) + (10 x $230) = $3,100; BS
    c. 36 x $450 = $16,200; IS
    d. $16,200 - 7,700 = $8,500; IS

    2. LIFO periodic:
    a. (10 x $230) + (20 x $220) + (6 x $210) = $7,960; IS
    b. (10 x $200) + (4 x $210) = $2,840; BS
    c. 36 x $450 = $16,200; IS
    d. $16,200 - 7,960 = $8,240; IS

    3. FIFO perpetual:
    a. (10 x $200) + (10 x $210) + (16 x $220) = $7,620; IS
    b. (10 x $230) + (4 x $220) = $3,180; BS
    c. $16,200 - 7,620 = $8,580; IS

4. FIFO periodic: same answers as in FIFO perpetual (3. above).

Weighted average periodic: Weighted average cost = $\dfrac{\text{cost of goods available for sale}}{\text{total snowboards available for sale}}$

$$= \dfrac{(10 \times \$200) + (10 \times \$210) + (20 \times \$220) + (10 \times \$230)}{10 + 10 + 20 + 10} = \dfrac{\$10,800}{50} = \$216 \text{ per snowboard}$$

   a. 36 snowboards x $216 = $7,776; IS
   b. (50 – 36) x $216 = $3,024; BS
   c. $16,200 - 7,776 = $8,424; IS

6. a. FIFO   The cost of snowboards has been rising. The FIFO method assumes the older, less expensive items are part of cost of goods sold. A lower cost of goods sold results in higher net income.

     b. LIFO   The cost of snowboards has been rising. The LIFO method assumes the newer, more expensive items are part of cost of goods sold. A higher cost of goods sold results in lower net income and lower income taxes.

     c. LIFO   Inventory turnover equals cost of goods sold divided by inventory. The cost of goods sold in the numerator is higher using LIFO, which assumes the newer, more expensive items are sold first, and the inventory in the denominator is smaller since the older, less expensive items are left in inventory.

     d. FIFO   The current ratio equals current assets divided by current liabilities. Inventory is a current asset. FIFO results in a higher inventory balance in times of rising prices than the other methods, because with FIFO the newer, more expensive items are left in inventory. Accounts payable is a current liability and would be the same balance, for the amount owed to the vendors, regardless of which method is used.

     e. FIFO   The gross margin on sales percentage equals the gross margin (or sales less cost of goods sold) divided by the sales. In times of rising prices, the FIFO method assumes the older, less expensive items are part of cost of goods sold. A lower cost of goods sold results in a higher gross margin. Since sales in the denominator is the same regardless of which inventory method is used, FIFO will result in the higher percentage.

Review Questions and Exercises

Completion Statements

Fill in the blank(s) to complete each statement.

1. The acquisition process is well controlled when a company requires the use of two documents: _____, and _____.

2. Purchase _____ and _____ reflect the amount of goods the company returned and price reductions the vendor allowed for defective goods kept by the company.

3. If the terms of purchase are _____, then the buyer pays the shipping cost. _____ is the cost paid by the purchasing company and is included in the buyer's cost of the goods.

4. If the terms of purchase are _____, then the seller pays the shipping cost. _____ is the delivery expense to the seller and is an operating expense on the seller's income statement.

5. When using the _____ method, the cost of goods sold equals the exact cost of the actual goods that have been sold. This method is the only method where the cost flow is the same as the physical flow of the goods.

6. When using the _____ method, a unit cost is calculated by dividing the total cost of goods available for sale by the total number of units available for sale.

7. The _____ method assumes the first goods purchased are sold first. Thus, the cost of goods sold is the cost of the older items and ending inventory is the cost of the most recent purchases.

8. The _____ method assumes the most recently purchased goods are sold first. Thus, the cost of goods sold is the cost of the newer items and ending inventory is the cost of the older items.

9. A _____ system records cost of goods sold and updates the inventory balance after every sale.

10. A _____ system records cost of goods sold and updates the inventory balance only at the end of each accounting period.

11. The formula for calculating the gross profit ratio is _____.

12. (Appendix 5B) The _____ provides a means of estimating inventory instead of actually counting the inventory. A company may use this method for estimating inventory for monthly or quarterly financial statements or for estimating lost inventory for insurance claims.

True/False

Indicate whether each statement is true (T) or false (F).

_____1. The purchase of inventory is recorded as an expense called cost of goods sold.

_____2. A company that uses the last-in, first-out method of valuing cost of goods sold must sell its newer inventory before selling any of its older inventory, even though some of the older items may be perishable.

_____3. A company that uses a perpetual inventory system must calculate cost of goods sold each time it records a sale.

_____4. Companies that use LIFO for federal income taxes must also use LIFO for financial reporting.

_____5. In a time of rising prices, a company that uses FIFO will have higher cash flow from operating activities than a company that uses LIFO.

_____6. Goods available for sale equals beginning inventory minus cost of goods sold.

_____7. A company has a gross profit ratio of 40%. This means that for every $1 of sales the company's cost of goods sold is $0.40.

_____8.   A car dealership will have a lower inventory turnover than a grocery store.

_____9.   (Appendix 5A) Cost of goods sold can be expressed as goods available for sale minus ending inventory.

_____10.   (Appendix 5B) The gross profit method is used to estimate cost of goods sold and ending inventory when the actual amounts are not available.

Multiple Choice

Select the best answer for each question.

_____1.   Inventory would be found in the:
    A. current liabilities section of the balance sheet.
    B. current assets section of the statement of financial position.
    C. operating section of the statement of operations.
    D. noncurrent assets section of the balance sheet.

_____2.   Which of the following accounting treatments violates the matching principle?
    A. A grocery store uses the LIFO cost flow method.
    B. Inventory is expensed in the period when it is sold.
    C. Inventory is expensed in the period when it is purchased.
    D. More than one of the above violates the matching principle.

_____3.   The lower-of-cost-or-market rule requires a company to:
    A. use the LIFO method in times of rising prices.
    B. adjust the inventory balance downward if its replacement cost is lower than its historical cost.
    C. adjust the cost of goods sold downward if the inventory's replacement cost is lower than its historical cost.
    D. use this method if its inventory has been destroyed or lost.

_____4.   The gross profit ratio for Proffits, Inc. increased from 45% in 2008 to 50% in 2009. Which of the following is **true**?
    A. Proffits made more sales in 2009 than in 2008.
    B. Proffits' net income was greater in 2009 than in 2008.
    C. Proffits' cost of sales was lower relative to sales in 2009 than in 2008.
    D. Proffits' markup on its goods was less in 2009 than in 2008.

_____5.   The excess of sales over cost of goods sold is:
    A. net income.
    B. income before taxes.
    C. operating income.
    D. gross profit.

_____6.   Redux, Inc. purchased $2,500 of inventory on account with terms of 2/10, n/30 and paid the bill within the discount period. How much did Redux pay?
    A. $2,500
    B. $2,450
    C. $2,300
    D. $2,250

_____7. FOB shipping point means the:
  A. purchaser pays the shipping costs and records an expense called freight-in.
  B. purchaser pays the shipping costs and records the cost as a part of inventory.
  C. seller pays the shipping costs and records an expense called freight-out.
  D. seller pays the shipping costs and records a contra-revenue account called freight-out.

_____8. Which of the following problems might explain an unusually high inventory turnover ratio?
  A. The inventory may be too low, causing goods to be out of stock and sales to be lost.
  B. The inventory may not be selling as quickly as it was in the past.
  C. The inventory may have been bought in quantities that are too large, causing goods to be on hand for too long.
  D. More than one of the above may be the cause of a high inventory turnover ratio.

_____9. In a time of rising prices, which inventory valuation method will report higher cost of goods sold?
  A. LIFO
  B. FIFO
  C. Weighted average
  D. This is a trick question. The choice of inventory valuation method has nothing to do with cost of goods sold.

_____10. In a time of **falling** prices, which inventory valuation method will report higher net income?
  A. LIFO
  B. FIFO
  C. Weighted average
  D. This is a trick question. The choice of inventory valuation method has nothing to do with net income.

_____11. (Appendix 5A) With a periodic inventory system, an undiscovered error that overstates the 2009 year-end inventory will cause an:
  A. overstatement of 2009 net income and an understatement of 2010 net income.
  B. understatement of assets on the 2009 balance sheet.
  C. overstatement of 2009 cost of goods sold.
  D. overstatement of 2009 net income and no effect on 2010 net income.

_____12. (Appendix 5B) If a company's inventory was destroyed by fire but the accounting records were saved, the method that would probably be used to estimate the amount of inventory lost would be the:
  A. LIFO method.
  B. weighted average cost method.
  C. gross profit method.
  D. specific identification method.

Exercises

For exercises 1. – 4., show the effect on the accounting equation. Include the proper account titles. Assume the company uses a perpetual inventory system.

1. On January 8, the company purchased $500 of inventory on account.

Assets	Liabilities	Shareholders' Equity	
		CC	Retained earnings

2. On February 8, the company paid the $500 invoice for merchandise previously purchased.

Assets	Liabilities	Shareholders' Equity	
		CC	Retained earnings

3. On February 9, the company sold merchandise to a customer on account for $400. The cost of the merchandise sold was $300.

Assets	Liabilities	Shareholders' Equity	
		CC	Retained earnings

4. On March 9, the company collected $400 of its accounts receivable.

Assets	Liabilities	Shareholders' Equity	
		CC	Retained earnings

5. Put an "X" in the column that indicates the best place to find each of the following items:

		Balance Sheet	Statement of Cash Flows	Income Statement	Notes to the Financial Statements
a.	The cost of inventory sold				
b.	The amount of merchandise on hand				
c.	The amount paid for inventory				
d.	The amount owed for inventory				
e.	The gross profit				
f.	The inventory method used				

6. Calculate the gross profit ratio and the inventory turnover ratio for the year ended December 31, 2009:

For the year ended	December 31, 2009	December 31, 2008
Inventory	$20,000	$30,000
Sales	$400,000	$380,000
Cost of goods sold	$180,000	$170,000

7. Stockit, Inc. has the following inventory information available from a recent month:

Date	Description	Units	Unit Cost / Price	Total
12/1	Beginning inventory	10	$10	$100
12/6	Purchase	20	$12	$240
12/18	Purchase	30	$16	$480
12/20	Sale	55	$30	$1,650
12/24	Purchase	10	$18	$180

Use the information above to complete the following table:

	Cost flow method:	Cost of goods sold	Ending inventory
a.	Perpetual LIFO		
b.	Periodic LIFO		
c.	Perpetual FIFO		
d.	Periodic FIFO		
e.	Periodic weighted average (round the unit cost to the nearest cent)		

8. (Appendix 5A) Put an "X" in the column that indicates whether the item is overstated, understated, or correctly stated as a result of a company overstating its December 31, 2008 inventory balance.

		Overstated	Understated	Correctly stated
a.	Inventory, January 1, 2008			
b.	Purchases during 2008			
c.	Goods available for sale in 2008			
d.	Inventory, December 31, 2008			
e.	Cost of goods sold in 2008			
f.	Net income in 2008			
g.	Retained earnings, December 31, 2008			
h.	Purchases during 2009			
i.	Goods available for sale in 2009			
j.	Inventory, December 31, 2009			
k.	Cost of goods sold in 2009			
l.	Net income in 2009			
m.	Retained earnings, December 31, 2009			

9. (Appendix 5B) S. Mates, Inc. filed an insurance claim for inventory destroyed by a storm. The inventory at the beginning of the year was $20,000. Purchases were $140,000 and sales were $240,000 for the year up to the storm. The gross profit percentage has historically been 45%. How much inventory should this company claim was lost?

Solutions to Review Questions and Exercises

Completion Statements

1. purchase requisition, purchase order
2. returns, allowances
3. FOB shipping point, Freight-in
4. FOB destination, Freight-out
5. specific identification
6. weighted-average
7. First-in, first-out (FIFO)
8. Last-in, first-out (LIFO)
9. perpetual
10. periodic
11. gross profit / sales or (sales – cost of goods sold) / sales
12. gross profit method

True/False

1. False   Inventory is a current asset until it is sold. When the inventory is sold, the cost of the sale is matched with the related sale in the same accounting period (the matching principle).
2. False   GAAP allows companies to select one of several inventory cost flow assumptions when determining the amount of cost of goods sold. The method used does not have to be consistent with the actual physical flow of the goods. Thus, a company that uses the LIFO method can physically sell its older inventory before its newly purchased items.
3. True
4. True
5. False   If a company uses FIFO, the oldest costs are used as cost of goods sold. When prices are rising, these old cost will be relatively low, resulting in a low cost of goods sold. Low cost means high income and high income taxes, which must be paid in cash. So a company that uses FIFO will pay more taxes and have less cash from operating activities.
6. False   Goods available for sale equals beginning inventory **plus** purchases.
7. False   The gross profit ratio of 40% means that for every $1 of sales, the cost of goods sold is $0.60 and the gross profit is $0.40.
8. True
9. True
10. True

Multiple Choice

1. **B**   Inventory is a current asset since it should be sold within the year. Another name for the balance sheet is the statement of financial position.

2. **C**   Inventory is an asset until it is sold. The matching principle requires the cost of the goods sold be reported in the same period as the related sale. The cost flow assumptions, such as LIFO and FIFO, are used to estimate the amount of cost of goods sold. GAAP allows companies to use estimates instead of tracking the actual physical flow and actual cost of each item sold.

3. **B**   Companies are required by GAAP to reduce the inventory balance downward if the historical cost of the inventory is higher than its market value, which is defined as replacement cost. This rule helps to prevent companies from overstating their inventory.

4. **C**   The gross profit ratio is calculated by dividing gross profit (or sales minus cost of goods sold) by sales. When the cost of goods sold is lower relative to sales, than the percentage increases since the numerator, gross profit, is larger. Choice A is incorrect because sales can increase at the same rate as cost of goods sold, causing the gross profit to remain the same. Choice B is incorrect because other operating expenses may have increased, offsetting any increase in the gross profit. Choice D is incorrect because a higher gross profit results when a company increases its markup on goods.

5. **D**   Sales minus cost of goods sold (or cost of sales) is the gross profit. It represents the markup on a company's goods.

6. **B**   The discount term, 2/10, n/30, means the buyer will receive a 2% discount if the invoice is paid within 10 days, otherwise the entire amount is due within 30 days. A 2% discount on $2,500 is $50. The buyer will pay $2,450 ($2,500 – 50).

7. **B**   FOB (free on board) shipping point means the purchaser pays the shipping costs. The shipping cost is considered part of the cost of buying the inventory and is included in inventory along with the purchase price. If the terms were FOB destination, then the shipper would pay and record the cost as an expense, freight-out.

8. **A**   The inventory turnover equals cost of goods sold divided by average inventory. If the inventory is low, the result would be a high turnover, which is typically good. However, if inventory is too low, the result would be loss of sales if the goods are temporarily out of stock. A low inventory turnover is usually not good and may be a result of not being able to sell the goods quickly enough and/or having too much inventory on hand.

9. **A**   LIFO uses the most recent prices as cost of goods sold. If prices are rising, LIFO will use the most recent, high prices as cost of goods sold.

10. **A**   LIFO uses the most recent prices as cost of goods sold. If prices are falling, LIFO will use the most recent, lower prices as cost of goods sold. Lower cost of goods sold means higher income.

11. **A**   Cost of goods sold is calculated by subtracting ending inventory from goods available for sale. If too much is subtracted as ending inventory, cost of goods sold will be too low. Low cost of goods sold results in high net income for 2009. In 2010, the high amount of beginning inventory increases the cost of goods available for sale. If the correct ending inventory for 2010 is subtracted from a number that is too large, cost of goods sold is too high for 2010 and net income is too low. Choice B is incorrect because assets on the balance sheet will be too large at the end of 2009. Choice C is incorrect because cost of goods sold in 2009 is too low, not too high. Choice D is incorrect because the error in 2009 ending inventory also has an effect on the income reported in 2010.

12. **C**   The gross profit method is the only method that can be used to calculate inventory without knowing the actual number of units in ending inventory. For both choices A and B, the number of units in inventory must be multiplied by the appropriate prices to calculate inventory cost. For Choice D, both the number of units and the actual cost of those units must be known.

Exercises

The effects of Exercises 1. – 4. on the accounting equation:

	Assets	Liabilities	CC	Shareholders' Equity — Retained earnings
1.	+500 Inventory	+500 Accounts payable		
2.	-500 Cash	-500 Accounts payable		
3.	+400 Accounts receivable -300 Inventory			+400 Sales -300 Cost of goods sold
4.	+400 Cash -400 Accounts receivable			

5.		Balance Sheet	Statement of Cash Flows	Income Statement	Notes to the Financial Statements
a.	The cost of inventory sold			X	
b.	The amount of merchandise on hand	X			
c.	The amount paid for inventory		X		
d.	The amount owed for inventory	X			
e.	The gross profit			X	
f.	The inventory method used				X

6.

$$\text{Gross profit ratio: } \frac{\text{gross profit}}{\text{sales}} = \frac{\$400,000 - 180,000}{\$400,000} = .55 \text{ or } 55\%$$

$$\text{Inventory turnover} = \frac{\text{Cost of goods sold}}{\text{Average inventory}} = \frac{\$180,000}{((\$20,000 + \$30,000)/2)} = 7.2 \text{ times}$$

7.	Cost flow method:	Cost of goods sold	Ending inventory
a.	Perpetual LIFO	(30 x $16) + (20 x $12) + (5 x $10) = $770	(5 x $10) + (10 x $18) = $230
b.	Periodic LIFO	(10 x $18) + (30 x $16) + (15 x $12) = $840	(10 x $10) + (5 x $12) = $160
c.	Perpetual FIFO	(10 x $10) + (20 x $12) + (25 x $16) = $740	(10 x $18) + (5 x $16) = $260
d.	Periodic FIFO	(10 x $10) + (20 x $12) + (25 x $16) = $740	(10 x $18) + (5 x $16) = $260
e.	Periodic weighted average $\frac{(\$100 + 240 + 480 + 180)}{(10 + 20 + 30 + 10)}$ $\frac{\$1,000 \text{ cost of goods available}}{70 \text{ units available for sale}}$ = $14.29 per unit (rounded)	55 x $14.29 = $785.95	$1,000 Cost of goods available for sale - $785.95 Cost of goods sold = $214.05

8.		Overstated	Understated	Correctly stated
a.	Inventory, January 1, 2008			X
b.	Purchases during 2008			X
c.	Goods available for sale in 2008			X
d.	Inventory, December 31, 2008	X		
e.	Cost of goods sold in 2008		X	
f.	Net income in 2008	X		
g.	Retained earnings, December 31, 2008	X		
h.	Purchases during 2009			X
i.	Goods available for sale in 2009	X		
j.	Inventory, December 31, 2009			X
k.	Cost of goods sold in 2009	X		
l.	Net income in 2009		X	
m.	Retained earnings, December 31, 2009			X

9. First estimate cost of goods sold:

Sales	100%	$240,000	
-Cost of goods sold	- 55%	132,000	((100% - 45%) x $240,000)
Gross profit	45%	$108,000	

Then estimate inventory:

Beginning inventory	$ 20,000
+ Purchases	140,000
Goods available for sale	$160,000
- Estimated cost of goods sold	(132,000) (see cost of goods sold above)
Estimated ending inventory	$ 28,000

CHAPTER 6
PAYMENT FOR GOODS AND SERVICES: CASH AND ACCOUNTS RECEIVABLE

Chapter Overview

Once the necessary assets, such as inventory, have been acquired, the company will want to sell its services or products and collect cash from its customers. Chapter 6 will help you to understand how to account for cash and accounts receivable and how this information is reported in the financial statements.

Chapter Highlights

1. Internal controls surrounding cash are important to help safeguard the cash and ensure that sales and cash collections are properly recorded. Controls include limiting access to the cash, segregating the duties of recordkeeping from custody of cash, and monitoring cash by preparing a **bank reconciliation**. A bank reconciliation, also known as a cash reconciliation, is a crucial control that compares the **bank statement** balance with the balance per the company's books and helps determine the company's true cash balance for the financial statements.

- A cash reconciliation is prepared as follows:

	Balance per bank statement	XX
+	Deposits in transit	XX
+	Bank errors in bank's favor	XX
-	Bank errors in company's favor	(XX)
-	Outstanding checks	(XX)
=	Correct (true) cash balance	XX

	Balance per books	XX
+	Notes collected by bank	XX
+	Interest earned	XX
+	Company errors in bank's favor	XX
-	Company errors in company's favor	(XX)
-	NSF checks	(XX)
-	Bank charges	(XX)
=	Correct (true) cash balance	XX

A bank reconciliation is prepared properly only if the correct (true) cash balances are the same coming from the bank to books and from the books to the bank. Any discrepancies must be investigated.

- The bank reconciliation does not directly affect the company's accounting records. Adjusting entries are required to adjust the cash balance per books to the correct (true) cash balance. All items needed to get the balance per books equal to the true cash balance require adjusting entries.

2. **Cash equivalents** are highly liquid investments with a maturity of three months or less that can be easily converted into a known amount of cash. Cash and cash equivalents is the first asset listed on the balance sheet and represents the amount on hand at the balance sheet date. The statement of cash flows explains the change in cash from one balance sheet date to the next.

3. **Accounts receivable**, also called receivables or trade receivables, are current assets arising from credit sales to customers. Unfortunately, a company cannot expect to collect 100% of its receivables. There are always some customers who do not pay. GAAP requires a company to estimate its uncollectible accounts. This estimated **bad debt expense** is matched with the same period as the related sales. This is called the **allowance method**. The adjusting entry required is:

Assets	Liab.	Shareholders' equity	
		CC	Retained earnings
- Allowance for un-collectible accounts			- Bad debts expense

The **allowance for uncollectible accounts** is a contra-asset account. Accounts receivable is not reduced directly because at the time of the adjusting entry the company is unable to determine exactly which accounts are not going to be collected. The allowance account represents only an estimate of uncollectible accounts. Accounts receivable less the

allowance for uncollectible accounts is called the carrying value or book value of accounts receivable and
represents the amount the company believes it will collect from its customers.

4. Under the allowance method, there are two ways to estimate the amount of uncollectible accounts, the percentage of sales method and the accounts receivable method. The adjusting entry is the same regardless of which method is used. It is the amount of the estimate that may differ.

- The **percentage of sales method** focuses on the income statement. Management estimates the bad debts expense as a percentage of credit sales. Notice the sales method ignores the unadjusted balance in the allowance for uncollectible accounts in estimating bad debts expense.

- The **accounts receivable method**, sometimes called the aging or percent of accounts receivable method, focuses on the balance sheet. Management analyzes accounts receivable by preparing an **aging schedule** of receivables. Based on this schedule, management estimates the percentage of accounts receivable that will not be collected. This method is more involved than the sales method because the amount of the adjustment depends on the unadjusted balance already in the allowance for uncollectible accounts.

5. The entry and amount to write off a specific customer's account will be the same regardless of which method is used.

Assets	Liab.	Shareholders' equity
+ Allowance for un- collectible accounts - Accounts receivable		

Notice the write-off of the specific account does not affect the net accounts receivable. The entry is reclassifying a previously unnamed bad debt to a named bad debt. Since the bad debts expense is only an estimate, each period the bad debts expense usually contains a little

adjustment for the over- or under-estimate from the previous period's entry.

6. The allowance method (using either the percentage of sales or accounts receivable methods) results in a better, more realistic measure of net income and accounts receivable than if the company were to wait until specific customers' accounts were determined to be uncollectible. Companies may ignore the allowance method only if their uncollectible accounts are very small. If they are immaterial, GAAP allows companies to use the **direct write-off method**. The company waits to write off a specific customer's account instead of making an adjusting entry for estimated bad debts in the same period as the related sales. This method violates the matching principle because the sale and the write-off of the uncollectible account may occur in different accounting periods. The write-off is recorded as:

Assets	Liab	Shareholders' equity	
		CC	Retained earnings
- Accounts receivable, J. Doe			- Bad debts expense

7. Credit card sales are not as risky as credit sales and are recorded as:

Assets	Liab	Shareholders' equity	
		CC	Retained earnings
+Accounts receivable (credit card company)			+Sales -Credit card expense

The credit card company, for a fee, will pay the company daily (or weekly):

Assets	Liab.	Shareholders' equity	
		CC	Retained earnings
+ Cash - Accounts receivable			

The company must compare the fee with the benefits of credit card sales such as having the credit card company pursue non-paying customers.

8. **Promissory notes**, or notes receivable, are promises by **makers** to pay a specified amount plus interest to the **payees** on specific dates. Interest is calculated as:

Interest = Principal x Rate x Time

Since the rate is an annual rate, the time must be expressed as a portion of a year if the note is a short-term note or if the period covered by the financial statements is less than a year.

9. When a company sells its product or service with a warranty, the matching principle requires the company to estimate and record warranty expense in the same period as the related sale:

Assets	Liabilities	Shareholders' equity	
		CC	Retained earnings
	+ Estimated warranty liability (or payable)		- Warranty expense

Later, the company will reduce this liability as it meets its warranty obligations to customers:

Assets	Liabilities	Shareholders' equity	
		CC	Retained earnings
- Cash *or* - Inventory	- Warranty payable		

10. Financial statements and related footnotes provide sales and accounts receivable information to help users assess a company's ability to collect its receivables and pay its obligations. Two ratios help to assess the company's ability to meet its short-term obligations: 1) the current ratio, which equals current assets divided by current liabilities, and 2) the quick (or acid-test) ratio, which equals cash plus short-term investments plus net accounts receivable in the numerator and current liabilities in the denominator. Another important ratio is the **accounts receivable turnover ratio,** which measures the company's ability to collect cash from its credit customers. It is calculated by dividing net sales by average net accounts receivable. This ratio can also be expressed as the average number of days it takes to collect for a sale by dividing the ratio into 365 days. The footnotes to the financial statements provide further detail about sales and collection policies.

14. Important internal controls are needed to help safeguard cash, accounts receivable and other assets and to ensure the financial records are accurate and reliable. Employees who have access to the physical assets should not have access to the accounting records. These employees should be given clear assignments of their responsibilities for controlling the assets. The procedures to be followed should be well documented. Lastly, the accounting data should be verified. For instance, requiring cashiers to give receipts to customers provides an independent internal control.

Featured Exercise

Part A. Fill in the accounting equation below for Tina'sWare, Inc.'s events that occurred during 2009.

Tina's Ware, Inc.	Assets =	Liabilities +	Shareholders' equity	
			Contributed capital	Retained earnings
Beginning balances, January 1, 2009	Cash 500 Accounts receivable 7,500 Allowance for uncol- lectible accounts (450) Inventory 5,000 Prepaid insurance 600 Truck (net) 16,000	Accounts payable 6,000 Interest payable 700 Notes payable 7,000	Common stock 6,000	Retained earnings 9,450
a	Purchased $32,000 of inventory on account			
b	Made sales of $55,000 on account; the cost of the sales was $35,000			
c	$49,000 of receivables were collected. A $1,000 account receivable was late and reclassified as a 3-month note receivable.			
d	Wrote off $400 of specific customer accounts considered uncollectible			
e	Paid $34,000 of its accounts payable			
f	Paid $2,400 in advance for an insurance policy that covers two years beginning July 1			
g	One year of insurance coverage has expired.			
h	Adjusting entries are $5 interest on the note receivable, $4,000 for depreciation and $700 for interest owed.			
i	In December, Tina's Ware began offering warranties and expects warranty costs on this year's sales to be $100.			
j	Tina's Ware uses the accounts receivable allowance method and estimates that 5% of its accounts receivable will be uncollectible.			

93

Part B: Tina's Ware's financial statement line items:		Fill in the correct dollar amount:	Put an "X" in the column of the statement where the item will most likely appear:		
		Amount as of or for the year ended December 31	**Income Statement**	**Balance Sheet**	**Statement of Cash Flows**
a.	Cash paid to suppliers				
b.	Accounts payable				
c.	Inventory				
d.	Cost of goods sold				
e.	Sales (net of sales discounts)				
f.	Cash received from customers				
g.	Accounts receivable				
h.	Allowance for uncollectible accounts				
i.	Bad debts expense				
j.	Notes receivable				
k.	Interest receivable				
l.	Warranty payable				
m.	Warranty expense				

Part C:

1. What should Tina's Ware record in January 2010 when a customer brings a product under warranty back to be fixed? The repair costs Tina's Ware $60.

Assets	Liabilities	Shareholders' equity	
		CC	Retained earnings

2. Assume Tina's Ware uses the sales method instead of the accounts receivable method to estimate bad debts expense. It believes 1% of its sales are uncollectible. What would be the adjusting entry?

Assets	Liabilities	Shareholders' equity	
		CC	Retained earnings

3. Calculate Tina's Ware's 2008 (not 2009) current ratio and quick ratio. The note payable and related interest are due in 2010.

4. Calculate Tina's Ware's 2009 (not 2008) accounts receivable turnover ratio. Do not include the $1,000 note receivable in the calculation.

5. When the bank statement is received each month, the cashier is required to adjust the cash balance in the accounting records to agree with the bank balance. Discuss the risk associated with this practice and suggest some internal controls that Tina's Ware should have in place.

Solution

Tina's Ware, Inc.

	Assets =	Liabilities +	Shareholders' equity	
			Contrib. cap.	Retained earnings
	Beginning balances, January 1, 2009	Cash 500 Accounts receivable 7,500 Allowance for uncol- lectible accounts (450) Inventory 5,000 Prepaid insurance 600 Truck (net) 16,000	Accounts payable 6,000 Interest payable 700 Notes payable 7,000	Common stock 6,000	Retained earnings 9,450
a	Purchased $32,000 of inventory on account	32,000 Inventory	32,000 Accounts payable		
b	Made sales of $55,000 on account; the cost of the sales was $35,000	55,000 Accounts receivable (35,000) Inventory			55,000 Sales (35,000) Cost of goods sold
c	$49,000 of receivables were collected. A $1,000 account receivable was late and reclassified as a 3-month note receivable.	49,000 Cash (50,000) Accounts receivable 1,000 Notes receivable			
d	Wrote off $400 of specific customer accounts considered uncollectible	400 Allowance for uncol- lectible accounts (400) Accounts receivable			
e	Paid $34,000 of its accounts payable	(34,000) Cash	(34,000) Accounts payable		
f	Paid $2,400 in advance for an insurance policy that covers two years beginning July 1	(2,400) Cash 2,400 Prepaid insurance			
g	One year of insurance coverage has expired.	(1,200) Prepaid insurance			(1,200) Insurance expense
h	Adjusting entries are $5 interest on the note receivable, $4,000 for depreciation and $700 for interest owed.	5 Interest receivable (4,000) Accumulated depreciation	700 Interest payable		5 Interest revenue (4,000) Depreciation expense (700) Interest expense
i.	In December, …expects warranty costs on this year's sales to be $100		100 Warranty payable		(100) Warranty expense
j.	Tina's Ware uses the accounts receivable allowance method and estimates that 5% of its accounts receivable will be uncollectible.	(555) Allowance for un- collectible accounts (see * below)			(555) Bad debts expense

* $7,500 + 55,000 - 50,000 - 400 = $12,100 Accounts receivable;

$12,100 x (5%) = $(605) adjusted Allowance for uncollectible accounts; $(450)+ 400 + X = $(605); X = (555)

95

Part B. Tina's Ware's financial statement line items:		Fill in the correct dollar amount: **Amount** as of or for the year ended December 31	Put an "X" in the column of the statement where the item will most likely appear:		
			Income Statement	**Balance Sheet**	**Statement of Cash Flows**
a.	Cash paid to suppliers	$(34,000)			X
b.	Accounts payable	$4,000		X	
c.	Inventory	$2,000		X	
d.	Cost of goods sold	$35,000	X		
e.	Sales	$55,000	X		
f.	Cash received from customers	$49,000			X
g.	Accounts receivable	$12,100		X	
h.	Allowance for uncollectible accounts	$(605) =$12,100 x(5%)		X	
i.	Bad debts expense	$555	X		
j.	Notes receivable	$1,000		X	
k.	Interest receivable	$5		X	
l.	Warranty payable	$100		X	
m.	Warranty expense	$100	X		

Part C:

1.	**Assets**	**Liabilities**	**Shareholders' equity**	
			CC	Retained earnings
	(60) Cash	(60) Warranty payable		

2.	**Assets**	**Liabilities**	**Shareholders' equity**	
			CC	Retained earnings
	(550) Allowance for uncollectible accounts *(1%) x $55,000 = $(550)*			(550) Bad debts expense

3. Current ratio = $\underline{\text{current assets}}$ = $\underline{\text{cash + accounts receivable (net) + inventory + prepaid insurance}}$
   (2008)   current liabilities   accounts payable

   = $\dfrac{\$500 + (7,500 - 450) + 5,000 + 600}{\$6,000}$ = 2.2

   Quick ratio = $\dfrac{\text{cash + accounts receivable (net)}}{\text{current liabilities}}$ = $\dfrac{\$500 + (7,500 - 450)}{\$6,000}$ = 1.3
   (2008)

4. A/R turnover = $\underline{\text{Net sales}}$ = $\dfrac{\$55,000}{\text{Average net AR ((\$7,500-450)+(12,100-605))/2}}$ = 5.9 times
   (2009)

5. The cashier could steal cash and then change the cash balance in the accounting records without being detected. An important internal control is the segregation of duties. The cashier, who handles the cash, should not have access to the accounting records. The record keeper should not have access to the cash. A bank reconciliation done correctly is a verification of the cash balance and should be performed by someone other than the cashier and record keeper. All the procedures and responsibilities of the employees should be well documented.

Review Questions and Exercises

Completion Statements

Fill in the blank(s) to complete each statement.

1. A _____ involves comparing the cash balance in the accounting records and the bank statement cash balance for the month.

2. Deposits made on the last day of the bank statement that did not reach the bank's record-keeping department in time to be included in the bank statement and are added to the bank balance are called _____ in _____.

3. _____ are highly liquid investments with a maturity of three months or less that a firm can easily convert into a known amount of cash.

4. GAAP requires companies to use the _____ to account for bad debts of customers instead of the direct write-off method.

5. The two methods of estimating bad debts expense are the _____ and the _____ methods.

6. The _____ represents the amount the company believes it will collect from its customers. This is also called the _____ value or _____ value of accounts receivable.

7. An _____ is an analysis of the amounts owed to a firm by the length of time they have been outstanding.

8. A difference between an account receivable and a note receivable is the note receivable requires the maker to pay both _____ and _____.

9. The _____ principle requires bad debts expense and warranty expense be recorded in the same period as the related sales.

10. A ratio that measures the company's ability to collect cash is calculated by dividing credit sales by average net accounts receivable and is called the _____ ratio.

True/False

Indicate whether each statement is true (T) or false (F).

_____1. The adjusting entry for bad debts is the same whether a company uses the direct write-off method or the sales method.

_____2. The quick ratio is a measure of a company's ability to pay its short-term obligations.

_____3. The lower the accounts receivable turnover ratio the longer it takes the company to collect its credit sales on average.

_____4. The adjusting entry to record warranty expense is recorded in the same period as the related sale instead of in a later period when the customer returns the defective merchandise.

_____5. The direct write-off method is better than the allowance method because it results in a better matching of bad debts expense with the related sales.

_____6. When using the sales method, bad debts expense equals the net sales times the percentage management considers uncollectible plus any balance already in the unadjusted Allowance for uncollectible accounts.

_____7. Bad debts expense will be higher for a company that accepts major credit cards rather than selling to customers on account using its own credit card.

_____8. An effective internal control procedure is to have the cashier count the cash in the cash drawer and record the sales in the accounting records.

_____9. The collection of an account receivable will cause the quick ratio to increase.

_____10. The matching principle requires bad debts expense be estimated and recorded in the period in which the sale is made, not in the period in which a specific receivable is later written off.

Multiple Choice

Select the best answer for each question.

_____1. The Allowance for uncollectible accounts on the balance sheet shows:
   A. how much a company wrote off as uncollectible during the period.
   B. how much a company recorded as bad debts expense during the period.
   C. the amount of receivables that a company believes it will not collect.
   D. the accumulation of all the uncollectible accounts since the beginning of the business.

_____2. Using the accounts receivable method, a company determines the allowance for uncollectible accounts should have an adjusted balance of $(1,000). Using the sales method, the company determines bad debt expense should equal $1,000. If the unadjusted balance of the allowance for uncollectible accounts is $(100), which allowance method would result in a larger decrease in shareholders' equity?
   A. accounts receivable method
   B. sales method
   C. Both a. and b. will result in the same decrease in shareholders' equity.
   D. Neither a. nor b. will result in a decrease in shareholders' equity.

_____3. Rite On, Inc. uses the allowance method and decided to write off an account receivable from I.M. Broke that is considered uncollectible. When Rite On writes off the account:
   A. total assets will increase.
   B. total assets will decrease.
   C. total assets will remain unchanged.
   D. retained earnings will decrease.

_____4. Which method will result in an allowance for uncollectible accounts account?
   A. accounts receivable method
   B. direct write-off method
   C. sales method
   D. Both A. and C. are correct.

_____5. Which method ignores the unadjusted balance in allowance for uncollectible accounts when recording the adjusting entry for bad debts expense?
   A. accounts receivable method
   B. direct write-off method
   C. sales method
   D. Both B. and C. are correct.

_____6. Which of the following is an effective segregation of duties in controlling cash? The employee who has access to cash should not:
   A. take the deposits to the bank.
   B. prepare the cash reconciliation.
   C. open the mail since it often includes checks.
   D. take sales orders from customers.

_____7. Collectibles, Inc. estimated that $20,000 of its receivables will be uncollectible based on an aging of its accounts receivable. Why then did Collectibles, Inc. record bad debts expense of only $18,000?
   A. Collectibles, Inc. purposely understated its expenses.
   B. Collectibles, Inc. had already written off $2,000 of its accounts receivable during the year.
   C. Collectibles, Inc. already had a $(2,000) balance in its allowance for uncollectible accounts.
   D. Collectibles, Inc. had underestimated its bad debts expense in the prior year.

_____8. The matching principle requires a company to:
   A. record the bad debts expense in the same period as the related sale.
   B. write off an uncollectible account in the period the account is found to be uncollectible.
   C. match the balance in the Allowance for uncollectible accounts with the Bad debts expense.
   D. match the Allowance for uncollectible accounts with the net realizable value of accounts· receivable.

_____9. Which one of the following items from a cash reconciliation does the company need to record in its accounting records?
   A. Deposits in transit
   B. NSF checks
   C. Outstanding checks
   D. None of the above because the company already has recorded these items before preparing its cash reconciliation.

_____10. Which of the following is true for a company that accepts credit cards?
   A. The company is more assured of collecting credit card sales.
   B. The company must compare the cost of the credit company's fees with the benefit of receiving cash sooner and the benefit of not needing to pursue non-paying customers.
   C. The company records a credit card expense when it records the related sale.
   D. All of the above are true.

Exercises

1. Complete the May 31, 2009 bank reconciliation for Well Balanced, Inc. given the following:

    a. Outstanding checks: No. 975...$1,260; No. 991...$300; No. 1073...$1,300
    b. Check no. 1018 (for repair expense) was written for $483 but erroneously recorded in Well Balanced's records as $843.
    c. Deposits in transit of $3,370
    d. NSF check from I.M. Broke of $440
    e. Bank service charge of $20

Well Balanced, Inc. Bank Reconciliation, May 31, 2009				
Balance per bank statement	$15,700		Balance per books	$16,310
Add:			Add:	
Deduct:			Deduct:	
True cash balance			True cash balance	

2. Which of the above reconciling items (a. - e.) require adjusting entries in Well Balanced's records?

3. Liquidators, Inc. uses the sales method in estimating bad debts expense and has found that such expense has consistently approximated 1% of net sales. At December 31 of the current year, accounts receivable total $100,000 and the allowance for uncollectible accounts has a $(300) balance prior to adjustment. Net sales for the current year were $800,000. The appropriate adjusting entry is:

Assets	Liabilities	Shareholders' equity	
		Contributed capital	Retained earnings

4. Macrohard, Inc., after aging its accounts receivable, estimated that 2% of its $125,000 receivables on hand would probably prove uncollectible. The allowance for uncollectible accounts contained a balance of $(300) before adjustments. The appropriate adjusting entry is:

Assets	Liabilities	Shareholders' equity	
		Contributed capital	Retained earnings

5. A customer used a credit card to purchase a $100 battery from Chargemup, Inc. What entry should Chargemup, Inc. record if the credit card company charges a 4% fee for its service?

Assets	Liabilities	Shareholders' equity	
		Contributed capital	Retained earnings

For Exercises 6. – 9., show the effect on the accounting equation by circling either increase, decrease, or no effect in each column.

6. The adjusting entry to record the estimate for warranty obligations is:

Assets	Liabilities	Total shareholders' equity
Increase	Increase	Increase
Decrease	Decrease	Decrease
No effect	No effect	No effect

7. The adjusting entry to record the estimate for bad debts expense is:

Assets	Liabilities	Total shareholders' equity
Increase	Increase	Increase
Decrease	Decrease	Decrease
No effect	No effect	No effect

6. The entry to record the collection of an account receivable is:

Assets	Liabilities	Total shareholders' equity
Increase	Increase	Increase
Decrease	Decrease	Decrease
No effect	No effect	No effect

9. The writing-off of a specific account receivable for a company that uses the allowance method is:

Assets	Liabilities	Total shareholders' equity
Increase	Increase	Increase
Decrease	Decrease	Decrease
No effect	No effect	No effect

10. Cycles, Inc.'s net credit sales for the current year are $6,000,000, and net accounts receivable at the beginning of the year was $700,000 and at the end was $800,000. Calculate the accounts receivable turnover. Also, calculate the average number of days its takes Cycles to collect its receivables (assume 365 days to a year).

Solutions to Review Questions and Exercises

Completion Statements

1. bank reconciliation
2. deposits, transit
3. Cash equivalents
4. allowance method
5. sales, accounts receivable
6. net receivables, carrying, book
7. aging schedule
8. principal, interest
9. matching
10. accounts receivable turnover

True/False

1. False   The direct write-off method does not require an adjusting entry for bad debts expense, thus it violates GAAP (the matching principle).
2. True
3. True
4. True
5. False   The allowance method (GAAP) is better than the direct write-off method (not GAAP).
6. False   The sales method estimates bad debts expense as net sales times the percentage management considers uncollectible. The balance left in the unadjusted allowance for uncollectible accounts is not part of the calculation. (However, it is part of the calculation of bad debts expense when a company uses the accounts receivable method).
7. False   The credit card company charges a fee because it takes on the risk of non-paying customers, relieving the company of bad debts expense.
8. False   Employees who have access to cash should not have any record-keeping responsibilities. Otherwise, an employee could steal cash and manipulate the bank reconciliation to conceal the theft.
9. False   The quick ratio will not be affected because both cash and accounts receivable are in the numerator. When accounts receivable is exchanged for cash the numerator is unchanged.
10. True

Multiple Choice

1. C   The allowance for uncollectible accounts, a contra-asset on the balance sheet, is subtracted from accounts receivable to show the net realizable value (the amount the company believes it will collect from its customers).
2. B   The accounts receivable method requires bad debts expense (which reduces shareholders' equity) to be only $900 since there is already a $(100) balance in the allowance account. The sales method does not consider what is left in the allowance account and thus the bad debts expense is the entire $1,000 estimate.

3. C The write-off of a specific account receivable has no effect on the net realizable value of receivables (accounts receivable minus allowance for uncollectible accounts) or on total assets:

Assets	Liabilities	Shareholders' equity	
		Contributed capital	Retained earnings
- Accounts receivable + Allowance for uncollectible accounts			

4. D The direct write-off method, which violates the matching principle, does not require an allowance account since no attempt is made to record the estimated amount of bad debts expense in the same period as the related sales. Accounts receivable are written off (expensed) in the period the receivables are considered uncollectible.

5. D The sales method's bad debts expense equals the percentage of sales management believes to be uncollectible times the credit sales; the adjusting amount is not dependent on the balance in the allowance account. The direct write-off method's bad debts expense is the actual amount of the specific accounts receivable written off; there is no allowance account needed with this method.

6. B Employees who have access to cash should not have any record-keeping responsibilities. Otherwise, an employee could steal cash and manipulate the cash reconciliation to conceal the theft.

7. C Management based its estimate on an aging of its accounts receivable and thus uses the accounts receivable method. The estimated $20,000 is the balance needed in the allowance for uncollectible accounts, not Bad debts expense. The bad debts expense amount is dependent on the unadjusted balance in the allowance for uncollectible accounts which must have had a $(2,000) unadjusted balance since the expense was only $18,000.

8. A The matching principle is extremely important for companies to follow since it results in net income being a more realistic, consistent, and comparable measure of profitability.

9. B The items in a bank reconciliation that require adjustment to the company's books are the items added or subtracted from the cash per the company's books to arrive at the true cash balance. These reconciling items include NSF checks and errors made by the company, collections made by the bank on the company's behalf, bank charges and interest earned.

10. D Credit card companies typically pay for credit card sales daily or weekly. The credit card company takes on the risk of non-paying customers, relieving the company of bad debts expense. The cost of the credit card sales is a fee that is recorded as an expense at the same time as the related credit card sale.

Exercises

1.	Well Balanced, Inc. Bank Reconciliation, May 31, 2009			
Balance per bank statement	$15,700		Balance per books	$16,310
Add:			Add:	
Deposits in transit	3,370		Correction of an error ($843-483)	360
Deduct:			Deduct:	
Check: no. 975	(1,260)		NSF check	(440)
Check no. 991	(300)		Bank service charge	(20)
Check no. 1073	(1,300)			
True cash balance	$16,210		True cash balance	$16,210

2. Which of the above reconciling items (a. - e.) require adjusting entries in Well Balanced's records?

> The error the company made (b), the NSF check (d), and the bank service charge (e) are all reconciling items that need to be recorded in Well Balanced's records.

3. Assets	Liabilities	Shareholders' equity	
		Contrib. cap.	Retained earnings
(8,000) Allowance for uncollectible accounts			(8,000) Bad debts expense *(1%) x $800,000*

4. Assets	Liabilities	Shareholders' equity	
		Contrib. cap.	Retained earnings
(2,200) Allowance for uncollectible accounts *((2%) x $125,000) + $300*			(2,200) Bad debts expense

5. Assets	Liabilities	Shareholders' equity	
		Contrib. cap.	Retained earnings
96 Accounts receivable			100 Sales (4) Credit card expense

	Assets	Liabilities	Total shareholders' equity
6.	No effect	Increase	Decrease
7.	Decrease	No effect	Decrease
8.	No effect	No effect	No effect
9.	No effect	No effect	No effect

10. $\text{AR turnover} = \dfrac{\text{Net sales}}{\text{Average net AR}} = \dfrac{\$6,000,000}{(\$700,000 + 800,000)/2} = 8 \text{ times per year}$

$\dfrac{365 \text{ days}}{\text{AR turnover}} = \dfrac{365}{8} = 45.6 \text{ days}$

CHAPTER 7
ACCOUNTING FOR LIABILITIES

Chapter Overview

This chapter discusses how companies use financing from creditors, both current and long-term, to buy assets and services. You will learn about accounting for payroll and long-term installment notes. You will also learn about bonds, which are a special type of long-term borrowing available to large companies.

Chapter Highlights

1. A liability is recorded in the accounting records when an obligation is incurred. Liabilities can be classified into three types. **Definitely determinable liabilities**, such as accounts payable, can be measured exactly. **Estimated liabilities**, such as warranty payable, have some uncertainty in the amount. **Contingent liabilities,** such as lawsuits and tax disputes, are potential obligations from past events that are not recorded as liabilities unless they are both probable and reasonably estimable.

2. Payroll is a common business expense that creates definitely determinable, current liabilities. The amount an employee earns (gross pay) is larger than his take-home pay (net pay). The difference is the taxes withheld from the employee's pay. The company is required by law to act as an agent for the government and send the money withheld to the proper authorities. These taxes include income taxes (FIT), Social Security taxes (FICA, currently 6.2% of gross pay) and Medicare taxes (currently 1.45% of gross pay). The employer is also required to match the amount of Social Security taxes and Medicare taxes.

3. An employee's paycheck affects a company's accounting equation as follows:

Assets	Liabilities	Sh. Equity	
		CC	RE
- Cash (net pay)	+ FIT payable + FICA payable + Medicare taxes payable		- Salary expense (gross pay)

When the company pays these taxes and pays the matching FICA and Medicare taxes, the effect on the accounting equation is:

Assets	Liabilities	Sh. Equity	
		CC	RE
- Cash	- FIT payable - FICA payable - Medicare taxes payable		- Payroll tax expense

3. **Short-term notes** are debts that are due in one year or less. **Long-term notes** like car loans are usually repaid with a series of equal installments over the life of the note. Some of each payment is interest and some is repayment of principal.

- Part of each installment payment decreases the outstanding principal of the loan. As the balance of the loan gets smaller, the interest for the next period gets smaller, too. Since the total amount of the installment payment stays the same, more of the next payment is used to repay loan principal because less of it is needed to cover interest.

- A **mortgage** is a special type of long-term note used to purchase property. It gives the lender a claim against the property until the loan is repaid.

- Payments on installment notes are calculated using the time value of money. A dollar received today is worth exactly $1. A dollar received a year ago is worth more than $1 today. It is worth the original dollar plus the interest that has been earned for the year gone by. A dollar received one year in the future is worth less than a dollar today. The $1 future receipt includes interest to compensate you for waiting. When you remove the interest, called **discounting** the future payment to calculate its value to you today (its **present value**), you have less than $1 today. The interest rate used in present value problems of this type is called the **discount rate**.

- Future installment payments on a loan include interest on any outstanding principal as well as part of the principal itself. The bank calculates the amount of compound interest it would receive over the life of the loan, adds it to the principal, and then figures the installment payments to be made. The discounted future installment payments, with interest removed, are equal to the amount being borrowed today, which is the present value of the loan.

4. Suppose you buy property by signing a $100,000, three-year, 8% mortgage note, with annual payments to be made at the end of each year. When the first installment payment of $38,803.35 is made, the interest component of this payment is $8,000 (**Interest = principal x rate x time,** or $100,000 x .08 x 1 year). The payment's effect on the accounting equation is:

Assets	Liabilities	Sh. Equity	
		CC	RE
(38,803.35) Cash	(30,803.35) Mortgage payable		(8,000) Interest expense

For the second year of the loan, the balance now owed on the mortgage is $69,196.65 ($100,000 – 30,803.35). When the second installment payment of $38,803.35 is made, the interest component of the payment is $5,535.73 ($69,196.65 x .08 x 1 year). The remaining $33,267.62 of the payment is applied to the loan principal, reducing the principal to $35,929.03 ($69,196.65 – 33,267.62).

When the final installment payment of $38,803.35 is made, the interest component of the payment is $2,874.32 ($35,929.03 x .08 x 1 year). The remaining $35,929.03 of the payment is applied to the loan principal, reducing the principal to zero.

Look at the amortization schedule in Exhibit 7-4 of your text. Each year the interest component of the loan payment is smaller because the loan principal is smaller, and more of each payment is used to repay principal.

5. Firms that need to borrow a lot of money may issue (*i.e.*, sell) **bonds**, which are written agreements to pay interest and to repay the buyers of the bonds (the lenders) at the end of the bonds' term. Companies issue bonds rather than borrowing from a bank because: 1) firms can borrow more money with bonds than with bank loans, 2) the time period for bonds may be 20 or 30 years, longer than the term usually available from banks, and 3) the interest rate on bonds is also usually lower than the interest rate on bank loans. Investors such as insurance companies and individuals buy bonds because there is a ready market, similar to the stock market, where they can sell their bonds at any time. Bond owners are creditors who have priority over stockholders, who are owners of the business. Bondholders may also get extra protection from **covenants** that are included in the bond agreement, such as limits on the issuing company's future borrowing or a requirement that the company maintain a particular current ratio.

6. The principal amount of a bond is also called the **face amount, face value, stated value,** or **par value**. Most bonds are issued in multiples of $1,000. The length of the loan period is the bonds' **maturity**. Most bonds pay the face value to bondholders at the **maturity date**. In the United States, bonds usually make semiannual interest payments based on the **stated rate** (also known as the **coupon rate**), which is the interest rate quoted on the face of the bonds.

7. There are different types of bonds. **Secured bonds** give the bondholder a claim to a specific company asset if there is a default (failure to meet the bond's obligations). Unsecured bonds, called **debentures**, are backed by the general credit of the company. **Term bonds** all mature on the same date. **Serial bonds** mature over a period of years. **Convertible** bonds can be exchanged for common stock whenever bondholders want. **Callable** bonds allow the issuing company to buy back a bond at any time before maturity at a price specified in the bond agreement. Some bonds, called **zero-interest** or **zero-coupon bonds**, do not make regular interest payments to bondholders because the stated rate of interest on these bonds is 0%. Instead, they make only a single payment of the bond's face value at maturity. Calculating the

issue price of these bonds is simply finding the present value of a single future cash receipt. These bonds sell at a big (deep) discount. **Junk bonds** are risky bonds that have been downgraded below investment grade to BB or below.

8. The selling price of a bond depends on the **market rate of interest**, which is the rate investors can earn on investments of similar risk. Investors will pay the present value of the bond's future cash flows, discounted at the market rate of interest. When market interest rates increase, a bond's price falls (and *vice versa*). This is because the bond's stated rate is fixed. If market interest rates have gone up and investors can earn a higher return elsewhere, the bond will be an unattractive investment unless the price of the bond goes down. Similarly, if the bond's stated interest rate is higher than the prevailing market rate of interest, investors will find the bond attractive and will bid up the price.

Bond prices are quoted as a percentage of face value:
- **Bonds issued at par** sell at 100, which stands for 100% of face value.
- **Bonds issued at a discount** sell for an amount less than face value and have a price below 100.
- **Bonds issued at a premium** sell for an amount greater than face value and have a price above 100.

9. When a company issues bonds, it records the cash received and the liability to repay the face value of the bonds, bonds payable. The periodic interest payments are calculated using the face amount of the bonds times the stated interest rate times the fraction of a year that has elapsed, even if the bonds sold for some amount other than the face value. The effect on the accounting equation is:

Assets	Lia.	Shareholders' equity	
		CC	RE
- Cash			- Interest expense

- Bonds sell at par only if the stated rate of interest is the same as the market rate of interest.

- When the stated interest rate is higher than the market rate of interest, the bonds will sell at a premium.

- When the stated interest rate is lower than the market rate of interest, the bonds will sell at a discount.

10. The price at which a bond is issued is equal to the present value of the future cash flows to be received by the bondholder, discounted at the market rate of interest.

1) Calculate the amount of the periodic interest payments: face value of the bond times the stated interest rate of the bond times the appropriate fraction of a year.

2) Calculate the present value of these future cash interest payments (the present value of an annuity).

3) Calculate the present value of the future payment of the bond's face value (the present value of a single amount).

4) Add the two present values together to determine the amount of cash the company will receive when the bond is issued.

If a $1,000, 6-year bond with annual interest payments of 5% was issued for $975.02 because the market rate of interest was 5.5%, the issuing company would record the discount as a separate, negative liability, called a contra-liability:

Assets	Liabilities		Sh. Eq.	
			CC	RE
975.02 Cash	1,000 (24.98)	Bonds payable Discount on bonds payable		

The balance sheet will show a long-term liability, bonds payable, at its net value or **carrying value**, which is face value net of (minus) the related discount.

If a $1,000, 6-year bond with annual interest payments of 5% was issued for $1,025.79 because the market rate of interest was 4.5%, the issuing company would record the premium as a separate liability, called an adjunct liability, which will be added to bonds payable on the balance sheet:

Assets	Liabilities		Sh. Eq.	
			CC	RE
1,025.79 Cash	1,000	Bonds payable		
	25.79	Premium on bonds payable		

11. Bond premiums and discounts are amortized, written off (reduced to zero) over the life of the bond issue. Interest expense shown on the company's annual income statement will not be the same amount as the cash interest payments made to bondholders.

Using the **effective interest method**, calculate interest expense by multiplying the carrying value of the bond times the market rate of interest in effect when the bond was issued times the appropriate fraction of a year. If a bond was issued at a discount, its carrying value, also called its net value or book value, is the amount of bonds payable minus the related discount on bonds payable. The difference between this interest expense and the actual interest payment made to bondholders (which is based on the face value, not the carrying value, and the stated interest rate, not the market interest rate) is the amount of the premium or discount to be amortized for the period.

Continue to use the example above of a $1,000, 6-year bond with annual interest payments of 5% that was issued for $975.02 because the market rate of interest was 5.5%. Interest expense for the first year would be:

$975.02 x 5.5% x 1 year = $53.63

However, the annual cash interest payment is:

$1,000 x 5% x 1 year = $50.00

The $3.63 difference between interest expense and the cash payment is the amount of the bond discount to be amortized.

The effect of the interest payment and discount amortization on the accounting equation is:

Assets	Liabilities		Sh. equity	
			CC	RE
(50) Cash	3.63	Discount on bonds payable		(53.63) Interest expense

As the bond discount is amortized, it becomes smaller. For the first year, $(24.98) + 3.63 = $(21.35). This means that less will be subtracted from the $1,000 balance in bonds payable and the carrying value of the bond increases ($1,000 – 21.35 = $978.65). At maturity, the discount will be zero and the carrying value of the bond will be equal to its $1,000 face value.

With the effective interest method, the interest expense shown on the income statement is based on the actual cash loaned to the company, $975.02, not the $1,000 face value of the bond. Interest expense also reflects the market rate of interest that investors demand, 5.5%, not the 5% stated rate. The cash interest payment made to bondholders, however, is less than the interest expense. The difference increases the carrying value of the bond, so that interest expense will be calculated for the second year on a greater principal amount, compounding interest on interest.

At maturity, bondholders receive the $1,000 face value of the bond, not the $975.02 they loaned the company. The difference between the two, the original unamortized discount of $24.98, can be thought of as extra interest that bondholders earn over the life of the bond issue, so that in effect they earn 5.5% on $975.02 rather than 5% on $1,000.

12. Bond premiums can also be amortized using the effective interest method. Go back to the earlier example of a $1,000, 6-year bond with annual interest payments of 5% issued for $1,025.79 when the market rate of interest was 4.5%. Interest expense in the first year would be:

$1,025.79 x 4.5% x 1 year = $46.16

However, the annual cash interest payment is:

$$\$1{,}000 \times 5\% \times 1 \text{ year} = \$50.00$$

The $3.84 difference between interest expense and the cash payment is the amount of the bond premium to be amortized. The effect of the interest payment and premium amortization on the accounting equation is:

Assets	Liabilities	Sh. equity	
		CC	RE
(50) Cash	(3.84) Premium on bonds payable		(46.16) Interest expense

As the bond premium is amortized, it becomes smaller. For the first year, $25.79 - 3.84 = $21.95. This means that less will be added to the $1,000 balance in bonds payable and the carrying value of the bond decreases ($1,000 + 21.95 = $1,021.95). At maturity, the premium will be zero and the carrying value of the bond will be equal to its $1,000 face value.

13. A second way to calculate the dollar amount of premium or discount to be amortized is to use the straight-line method. Simply divide the total premium or discount by the number of interest payment periods. An equal amount of premium or discount will be amortized each period. Straight-line amortization is easy, but it is not GAAP. However, it is allowed if the resulting interest expense and carrying value of bonds payable are not significantly different from those calculated using the effective interest method.

14. A company's **capital structure** is the mix of debt and equity that it uses to finance its assets. Borrowing money is a good idea for a company if the benefit to the company is greater than the cost of borrowing. This means the company has positive **financial leverage**, which is using borrowed money to increase earnings.

The **debt-to-equity ratio** compares the value of creditors' claims to the value of owners' claims. It is calculated as:

$$\frac{\text{Total liabilities}}{\text{Total shareholders' equity}}$$

A company with a high ratio is referred to as highly leveraged.
The **times-interest-earned ratio** measures a company's ability to make its interest payments:

$$\frac{\text{Income from operations}}{\text{Interest expense}}$$

A company with a low times-interest-earned ratio may have too much debt.

Details about a company's long-term debt are usually found in the notes to its financial statements.

15. Debt carries risk for both the issuing company and its creditors, which is the risk that the company will not meet its obligations. A company can reduce its risk by 1) a thorough cost-benefit analysis of any intended long-term borrowing to determine if it will earn more than it costs, and 2) studying the characteristics such as interest rates, borrowing terms, and ease of obtaining money for different types of borrowing available.

16. Off-balance-sheet financing occurs when a firm structures a transaction so that debt does not appear on its balance sheet. It is not always unethical or a violation of GAAP, but some major frauds, such as Enron, have involved off-balance-sheet financing.

17. (Appendix 7A) Simple interest is calculated on only the principal of a loan. Compound interest is calculated on the principal plus any interest that has been earned but not yet collected or paid. Money invested at compound interest grows much faster than money invested at simple interest, because with compound interest the amount on which interest is calculated gets bigger each year.

18. A payment of $100 received a year from today has a present value of less than $100. The present value today, plus the interest it earns for one year, equals $100. You can find the present value of a single sum using the formula:

$$PV = FV_n \times \frac{1}{(1+i)n}$$

You can also find the present value of a future amount using *The Present Value of $1* table in Appendix 7A of your textbook. The interest rate used in present value problems is called the discount rate.

There are instructions in appendix 7A of your textbook for finding the present value of a single amount using a financial calculator.

19. An **annuity** is a series of payments where the dollar amount of each payment is the same, and the time period between payments is also the same. With an **ordinary annuity,** the investor makes payments at the end of each time period.

Interest rates quoted by lenders are usually annual interest rates. If interest is compounded more than once a year, both the interest rate (i) and the number of periods (n) must be adjusted. If 6% interest is compounded monthly (12 times a year) for three years, then use a 0.5% interest rate (6% divided by 12 compoundings per year) for 36 periods (three years times 12 payments per year).

- You can calculate the present value of an annuity by finding the present value of each

payment separately, then adding them together.

- You can use *The Present Value of an Annuity* table found in Appendix 7A of your textbook.

- You can use a financial calculator, following the instructions in your textbook.

20. The present value of a series of installment loan payments is the same as the principal amount. To calculate the dollar amount of installment payments, first make sure that the annual interest rate and number of time periods are adjusted to fit the payment schedule. If payments are made monthly, the annual interest rate must be divided by 12 and the number of years must be multiplied by 12. The amount being borrowed, the loan's present value, is equal to the unknown future installment payments times the appropriate factor from the *Present Value of an Annuity* table. Divide the loan principal by the appropriate factor from the table and your answer is the amount of each installment payment. You can also use a financial calculator, following the instructions given in your textbook.

Featured Exercise

A company needs to borrow $1,000,000 to finance a major expansion. One financing alternative is a ten-year bank loan with an annual interest rate of 8%. Annual payments will be $149,029.52.

Part A: Prepare an amortization schedule for the loan.

Mortgage balance		Annual payment	Interest portion of payment	Amount of mortgage reduction
Beginning balance $1,000,000	1st			
After 1st payment	2nd			
After 2nd payment	3rd			
After 3rd payment	4th			
After 4th payment	5th			
After 5th payment	6th			
After 6th payment	7th			
After 7th payment	8th			
After 8th payment	9th			
After 9th payment	10th			
After 10th payment 0				

Part B: Now assume that the company decides instead to issue $1,000,000 of ten-year, 6.5% mortgage bonds to finance the expansion. The bonds will pay interest annually.

1. If the market rate of interest is 7%, these bonds will sell at (**circle one**):
     a premium   a discount   par

2. How much cash will the company pay on each interest payment date? _____

3. How much cash will the company pay when the bonds mature? Assume the last interest payment has already been made separately. _____

4. Calculate the amount of cash the company will receive when it issues the bonds.

5. Check your answers to questions 1 through 4, then complete the amortization schedule for the first four years of the bond issue using the effective interest method.

	Beginning carrying value	Cash payment	Interest expense	Amortization of discount	Ending carrying value
Year 1					
Year 2					
Year 3					
Year 4					

6. At maturity, the unamortized discount on the bonds will be _____ and the carrying value of the bonds will be _____.

7. If the market rate of interest is 6%, these bonds will sell at (circle one):
    a premium   a discount   par

8. How much cash will the company pay on each interest payment date? _____

9. How much cash will the company pay when the bonds mature? Assume the last interest payment has already been made separately. _____

10. Calculate the amount of cash the company will receive when it issues the bonds.

11. Check your answers to questions 7 through 10, then complete the amortization schedule for the first four years of the bond issue using the effective interest method.

	Beginning carrying value	Cash payment	Interest expense	Amortization of premium	Ending carrying value
Year 1					
Year 2					
Year 3					
Year 4					

12. At maturity, the unamortized premium on the bonds will be _____ and the carrying value of the bonds will be _____.

Solution

Mortgage balance		Annual payment	Interest portion of payment	Amount of mortgage reduction
Beginning balance $1,000,000	1st	$149,029.52	$80,000.00 *1,000,000 x .08*	$69,029.52 *149,029.52 – 80,000.00*
After 1st payment	930,970.48 *1,000,000 – 69,029.52* / 2nd	$149,029.52	74,477.64 *930,970.48 x .08*	74,551.88 *149,029.52 – 74,477.64*
After 2nd payment	856,418.60 *930,970.48- 74,551.88* / 3rd	$149,029.52	68,513.49 *856,418.60 x .08*	80,516.03 *149,029.52 – 68,513.49*
After 3rd payment	775,902.57 *856,418.60 - 80,516.03* / 4th	$149,029.52	62,072.21 *775,902.57 x .08*	86,957.31 *149,029.52 – 62,072.21*
After 4th payment	688,945.26 *775,902.57- 86,957.31* / 5th	$149,029.52	55,115.62 *688,945.26 x .08*	93,913.90 *149,029.52 – 55,115.62*
After 5th payment	595,031.36 *688,945.26 - 93,913.90* / 6th	$149,029.52	47,602.51 *595,031.36 x .08*	101,427.01 *149,029.52 – 47,602.51*
After 6th payment	493,604.35 *595,031.36 - 101,427.01* / 7th	$149,029.52	39,488.35 *493,604.35 x .08*	109,541.17 *149,029.52 – 39,488.35*
After 7th payment	384,063.18 *493,604.35 - 109,541.17* / 8th	$149,029.52	30,725.05 *384,063.18 x .08*	118,304.47 *149,029.52 – 30,725.05*
After 8th payment	265,758.71 *384,063.18 - 118,304.47* / 9th	$149,029.52	21,260.70 *265,758.71 x .08*	127,768.82 *149,029.52 – 21,260.70*
After 9th payment	137,989.89 *265,758.71 - 127,768.82* / 10th	149,029.08 *	11,039.19 *137,989.89 x .08*	137,989.89
After 10th Pmt.	0			

* The final payment is adjusted to equal the balance due on the mortgage plus the last year's interest ($137,989.89 + 11,039.19)

Part B:
1. a discount
2. $65,000 ($1,000,000 x .065 x 1 year)
3. $1,000,000
4. First, find the present value of the series of ten future interest payments of $65,000 each, discounted at the 7% market rate of interest: $65,000 x 7.02358 = $456,532.70
   Then find the present value of the single payment of $1,000,000 face value ten years from now at maturity, discounted at the 7% market rate of interest: $1,000,000 x 0.50835 = $508,350.00.
   Finally, add the two together: $456,532.70 + 508,350.00 = $964,882.70

5.	Beginning carrying value	Cash payment	Interest expense	Amortization of discount	Ending carrying value
1	$964,882.70	$65,000.00 *1,000,000 x .065*	$67,541.79 *964,882.70 x .07*	$2,541.79 *67,541.79 - 65,000*	967,424.49 *964,882.70 + 2,541.79*
2	967,424.49	65,000.00	67,719.71 *967,424.49 x .07*	2,719.71 *67,719.71 - 65,000*	970,144.20 *967,424.49 + 2,719.71*
3	970,144.20	65,000.00	67,910.09 *970,144.20 x .07*	2,910.09 *67,910.09 - 65,000*	973,054.29 *970,144.20 + 2,910.09*
4	973,054.29	65,000.00	68,113.80 *973,054.29 x .07*	3,113.80 *68,113.80 - 65,000*	976,168.09 *973,054.29 + 3,113.80*

6. At maturity, the unamortized discount on the bonds will be $0 and the carrying value of the bonds will be $1,000,000.
7. a premium
8. $65,000 ($1,000,000 x .065 x 1 year)
9. $1,000,000
10. First, find the present value of the series of ten future interest payments of $65,000 each, discounted at the 6% market rate of interest: $65,000 x 7.36009 = $478,405.85.
    Then find the present value of the single payment of $1,000,000 face value ten years from now at maturity, discounted at the 6% market rate of interest: $1,000,000 x 0.55839 = $558,390.00.
    Finally, add the two together: $478,405.85 + 558,390.00 = $1,036,795.85.

11.	Beginning carrying value	Cash payment	Interest expense	Amortization of premium	Ending carrying value
1	$1,036,795.85	$65,000.00 *1,000,000 x .065*	$62,207.75 *1,036,795.85 x .06*	$2,792.25 *65,000 – 62,207.75*	$1,034,003.60 *1,036,795.85 - 2,792.25*
2	1,034,003.60	65,000.00	62,040.22 *1,034,003.60 x .06*	$2,959.78 *65,000 - 62,040.22*	1,031,043.82 *1,034,003.60 - 2,959.78*
3	1,031,043.82	65,000.00	61,862.63 *1,031,043.82 x .06*	3,137.37 *65,000 - 61,862.63*	1,027,906.45 *1,031,043.82 - 3,137.37*
4	1,027,906.45	65,000.00	61,674.39 *1,027,906.45 x .06*	3,325.61 *65,000 - 61,674.39*	1,024,580.84 *1,027,906.45- 3,325.61*

12. At maturity, the unamortized premium on the bonds will be $0 and the carrying value of the bonds will be $1,000,000.

Review Questions and Exercises

Completion Statements

Fill in the blank(s) to complete each statement.

1. There are two types of liabilities: _____, such as accounts payable, can be measured exactly; _____, such as warranty payable, have some uncertainty in the amount.

2. The amount an employee earns is called _____. His take-home pay is called _____

3. Employers are required by law to withhold _____, _____, and _____ from their employees.

4. A _____ is a special type of long-term note used to purchase property. It gives the lender a claim against the property until the loan is repaid.

5. Removing the interest from a future payment to calculate its present value is called _____. The interest rate used in present value problems of this type is called the _____.

6. Bondholders may get extra protection from _____ included in the bond agreement. These might place limits on the issuing company's future borrowing or require the company to maintain a particular current ratio.

7. Most bonds pay the face value to bondholders at the _____.

8. Unsecured bonds, called _____, are backed by the general credit of the company.

9. _____ bonds all mature on the same date, while _____ bonds mature over a period of years.

10. The formula for calculating the debt-to-equity ratio is _____.

11. The formula for calculating the times-interest-earned ratio is _____.

12. (Appendix) A series of payments where the dollar amount of each payment is the same and the time period between payments is also the same is called an _____.

True/False

Indicate whether each statement is true (T) or false (F).

_____ 1. Employers are required to match the amount of social security they withhold from their employees.

_____ 2. Employers are required to match the amount of federal income tax they withhold from their employees.

_____ 3. Gross pay is larger than net pay.

115

_____ 4. If the market rate of interest is higher than a bond's stated rate, the bond will sell at a premium.

_____ 5. A low times-interest-earned ratio may mean a company is having difficulty making its interest payments.

_____ 6. A company that is highly leveraged has very little debt.

_____ 7. If a company issues bonds at a discount, interest paid to bondholders during the period will be more than the interest expense shown on the company's income statement.

_____ 8. The carrying value of a bond sold at a premium is the face value of the bond plus the related premium.

_____ 9. Assume that a long-term note payable will be repaid with five equal annual installment payments. Interest expense reported from this loan will be the same for each of the five years.

_____ 10. At maturity, the discount on a bond sold below par is zero.

Multiple Choice

_____ 1. Bonds sell at par when the coupon rate is _____ the market rate of interest.
   A. higher than
   B. lower than
   C. the same as
   D. The answer cannot be determined from the information given.

_____ 2. _____ bonds can be exchanged for common stock whenever bondholders want.
   A. Convertible
   B. Callable
   C. Serial
   D. Term

USE THE FOLLOWING INFORMATION TO ANSWER THE NEXT SEVEN QUESTIONS:
On January 1, 2009, Debtor Corporation issued $2,000,000 of 20-year, 8% bonds at 96, when the market rate of interest was 8.5%. The bonds pay interest annually on December 31. The company uses the effective interest method of amortization.

_____ 3. These bonds sold at:
   A. a premium.
   B. a discount.
   C. par.
   D. term.

_____ 4. How much cash did Debtor Corporation receive when the bonds were issued?
   A. $960,000
   B. $1,920,000
   C. $2,000,000
   D. $1,840,000

_____ 5. How much cash will bondholders receive when the bonds mature? (Assume that the final payment of interest has already been made separately.)
   A. $60,000
   B. $1,920,000
   C. $2,000,000
   D. $1,840,000

_____ 6. How much cash will bondholders receive on December 31, 2009, the first interest payment date?
   A. $160,000
   B. $170,000
   C. $153,600
   D. $163,200

_____ 7. How much interest expense will Debtor Corporation report on its income statement for the year ended December 31, 2009?
   A. $160,000
   B. $170,000
   C. $153,600
   D. $163,200

_____ 8. With each annual payment of bond interest, the net value (or carrying value) of the bonds will:
   A. increase.
   B. decrease.
   C. remain the same.
   D. change in a way that cannot be predicted because it depends on the market rate of interest in effect at the end of each year.

_____ 9. With each annual payment of bond interest, the interest expense reported for the year will:
   A. increase.
   B. decrease.
   C. remain the same.
   D. change in a way that cannot be predicted because it depends on the market rate of interest in effect at the end of each year.

_____ 10. Bonds that make no annual interest payments to investors, but instead pay only the face value of the bonds at maturity, are:
   A. convertible bonds.
   B. serial bonds.
   C. premium bonds.
   D. zero-interest or zero-coupon bonds.

Exercises

1. On January 1, a company borrowed $40,000 at 11% interest. The loan will be repaid with four equal annual installment payments of $2,893 made on the last day of each year.

Complete the amortization schedule for the loan. Round your answers to the nearest dollar.

Mortgage balance		Annual payment	Interest portion of payment	Amount of Mortgage reduction
Beginning balance $40,000	1st			
After 1st payment	2nd			
After 2nd payment	3rd			
After 3rd payment	4th			
After 4th payment 0				

2. Check your answers for the amortization table above, then answer the questions below. Fill in the correct dollar amount and circle the statement on which it appears, using the following code:
IS is the income statement for the year described
BS is the balance sheet at the end of the year described
SOCF is the statement of cash flows for the year described

a. For Year 1, interest expense of $_____ appears on the   IS   BS   SOCF

b. For Year 1, cash paid for interest of $_____ appears on the   IS   BS   SOCF

c. For Year 1, notes payable of $_____ appears on the   IS   BS   SOCF

d. For Year 1, cash paid for loan principal of $_____ appears on the   IS   BS   SOCF

e. For Year 2, cash paid for loan principal of $_____ appears on the   IS   BS   SOCF

f. For Year 2, notes payable of $_____ appears on the   IS   BS   SOCF

g. For Year 2, interest expense of $_____ appears on the   IS   BS   SOCF

h. For Year 2, cash paid for interest of $_____ appears on the   IS   BS   SOCF

3. On January 21, 2009, the company's gross payroll for the pay period is $8,000. The taxes withheld include federal income taxes withheld of $1,600, Social Security taxes of 6.2%, and Medicare taxes of 1.45%. The company will not deposit payment for these taxes until February. Show the effect on the accounting equation, including both account titles and dollar amounts.

Assets	Liabilities	Shareholders' Equity	
		CC	Retained earnings

4. On February 1, 2009, the company recorded its payroll tax expense and payment of taxes owed from 3. above. Show the effect on the accounting equation, including both account titles and dollar amounts.

Assets	Liabilities	Shareholders' Equity	
		CC	Retained earnings

Solutions to Review Questions and Exercises

Completion Statements

1. definitely determinable, estimated
2. gross pay, net pay
3. federal income tax (FIT), Social Security (FICA), Medicare tax
4. mortgage
5. discounting, discount rate
6. covenants
7. maturity date
8. debentures
9. Term, serial
10. total liabilities divided by total shareholders' equity
11. income from operations divided by interest expense
12. annuity

True/False

1. True
2. False   Only Social Security and Medicare are matched by the employer.
3. True
4. False   If the market rate of interest is higher for other investments, investors will refuse to buy the bond unless the price is less than face value. The bond will sell at a discount.

5. True
6. False Financial leverage is using borrowed money to increase earnings. A highly leveraged company has a lot of debt.
7. False If the bond was sold at a discount, the stated interest rate on the bond must be lower than the market rate of interest in effect when the bond was issued. Using the effective interest method, interest expense on the income statement will reflect the higher, market interest rate, and be more (not less) than the cash paid for interest. Part of the current period's interest expense is paid to bondholders in cash, and the remainder is added to the carrying value of the discounted bond, to be paid to bondholders at maturity.
8. True
9. False Part of each of the five installment payments is interest and part is principal. Since each of the payments makes the principal smaller, interest expense will be calculated on a smaller principal amount each period. Interest expense decreases with each successive payment, even though the total amount of the payment stays the same.
10. True

Multiple Choice

1. C The law of supply and demand determines prices in the bond market. If the coupon interest rate is higher than the market interest rate, the rate investors can earn elsewhere, they will see the bond as a good investment and drive the price up above par. If the coupon interest rate is lower than the market interest rate, investors will not buy the bond unless the price is less than face value.
2. A If the bonds are convertible, bondholders can exchange their bonds for stock at any time. The issuing company is allowed to buy back callable bonds whenever it wants. Term bonds all mature on the same date, while serial bonds mature over a period of years.
3. B The price at which the bonds were issued is 96, which means 96% of face value. Since investors could earn the 8.5% market rate of interest elsewhere, they will not buy the bonds unless the price drops below par.
4. B 96% x $2,000,000 = $1,920,000
5. C Bondholders receive the full $2,000,000 face value of the bonds at maturity, regardless of the price that they paid for the bonds
6. A Interest payments are determined by the terms of the bond contract ($2,000,000 x .08 x 1 year).
7. D Using the effective interest method, interest expense is based on the carrying value (or net value) of the bond, times the effective interest rate when the bonds were issued, times the appropriate fraction of a year ($1,920,000 x .085 x 1 year).
8. A Each year the discount on bonds payable will decrease by the difference between interest expense and the cash paid for interest. As the discount on bonds payable becomes smaller, less is subtracted from the face value of the bonds, and the net value becomes larger.
9. A Using the effective interest method, interest expense is based on the carrying value (or net value) of the bond, times the effective interest rate when the bonds were issued (not the rate in effect at the end of each year). As the carrying value of the bonds increases from year to year, the interest expense will increase, too.
10. D Since the annual interest payment is based on the stated interest rate times the face value of the bond, a zero-coupon bond, which has a stated interest rate of 0%, does not make annual interest payments to bondholders.

Exercises

Mortgage balance			Annual payment	Interest portion of payment	Amount of Mortgage reduction
Beginning balance	$40,000	1st	$12,893	$4,400 _40,000 x .11_	$8,493 _12,893 - 4,400_
After 1st payment	31,507 _40,000 - 8,493_	2nd	12,893	3,466 _31,507 x .11_	9,427 _12,893 –3,466_
After 2nd payment	22,080 _31,507 - 9,427_	3rd	12,893	2,429 _22,080 x .11_	10,464 _12,893 – 2,429_
After 3rd payment	11,616 _22,080 - 10,464_	4th	12,894 _11,616+1,278_	1,278 _11,616 x .11_	11,616*
After 4th payment	0				

* The final loan payment has been adjusted to pay off the principal balance completely, plus interest for the fourth year.

2. a. $4,400   IS
   b. $4,400   SOCF
   c. $31,507   BS
   d. $8,493   SOCF
   e. $9,427   SOCF
   f. $22,080   BS
   g. $3,466   IS
   h. $3,466   SOCF

3.

Assets	Liabilities	Shareholders' Equity	
		CC	**Retained earnings**
(5,788) Cash	1,600 FIT payable 496 FICA payable 116 Medicare taxes payable		(8,000) Salary expense

4.

Assets	Liabilities	Shareholders' Equity	
		CC	**Retained earnings**
(2,824) Cash	(1,600) FIT payable (496) FICA payable (116) Medicare taxes payable		(612) Payroll tax expense

CHAPTER 8
Accounting for Shareholders' Equity

Chapter Overview

When a business begins or wants to expand, it needs to obtain financing. The two sources of financing are debt financing (money from creditors), and equity financing (money from owners). Chapter 7 helps you to understand debt financing. Chapter 8 will help you to understand equity financing. You will see how the money a corporation receives from its owners, called stockholders, is obtained and shown on the financial statements. You will also see how the corporation reports its earnings and its distributions of these earnings to stockholders on the financial statements.

Chapter Highlights

1. All companies, whether they are sole proprietorships, partnerships, or corporations, receive contributions from owners. Corporation owners are called stockholders or shareholders. Shareholders' equity represents these owners' claims to the assets after the liabilities have been paid. Shareholders' equity is made up of **contributed capital** (owners' contributions) and **retained earnings** (earnings kept by the business). Contributed capital (or paid-in capital) is divided into two parts, **capital stock** and **additional paid-in capital**, that together represent the amount received from owners in cash (or sometimes other assets, like property).

2. To begin, a corporation must receive a corporate charter from the state where the firm is located. The charter authorizes the maximum number of shares a corporation is allowed to issue (sell). The number of shares a company issues cannot exceed the number authorized. All corporations have **common stock** which has specific rights: 1) to vote for members of the board of directors; 2) to share in the corporation's profits; 3) to share in any assets left if the corporation is to dissolve; and 4) to buy more shares when the corporation issues new stock.

- The amount of common stock equals the number of shares issued times the par value of the common stock. The **par value** is an arbitrary fixed per-share amount stated on the stock certificate. Par value has no real meaning in today's business environment, and most states do not require a par value. The state and/or corporate charter also defines the minimum amount of capital the company must maintain in order to protect creditors. If shareholders' equity falls below this minimum amount, the company is restricted from paying dividends.

- The par value is not to be confused with the market price the stock sells for when issued. The par value is typically much lower than the market price. The difference between the market price (the value received from the shareholder) and the par value, when the stock is issued, is called **additional paid-in capital** or **paid-in capital in excess of par**.

3. Shareholders take risks in hope of receiving cash **dividends** and an increase in the stock's market value. The board of directors determines how much and when a dividend will be paid and are not legally obligated to do so until the dividend is declared.

- The declaration date is the date the board of directors decides a dividend will be paid. A legal liability is created and recorded as:

Assets	Liabilities	Shareholders' equity	
		Contributed capital	Retained earnings
	+ Dividends payable		- Dividends

- The record date determines who will receive the dividends. Stocks are frequently traded on the stock market, so whoever owns the stock on the record date will receive the full dividend (even if the new stockholder held the stock for only one day). After this date, the stock is said to trade ex-dividend.

- The payment date is when the cash is actually paid to the shareholders. The effect on the accounting equation is to reduce assets (cash) and reduce liabilities (dividends payable).

4. Some corporations issue **preferred stock** that has preference over common stock for dividends and claims on assets if the corporation were to dissolve. Common stockholders, however, typically have other rights that preferred stockholders do not, such as voting rights and the right to receive new shares of stock.

- The amount of dividends a preferred stockholder receives equals the dividend rate times the par value stated on the preferred stock. The dividends remaining, after the preferred stock dividends have been met, go to the common stockholders.

- There are two types of preferred stock. **Cumulative preferred stock** means the dividend accumulates so that no common stockholder can receive dividends until all past, unpaid dividends (**called dividends in arrears**) have been paid to the cumulative preferred stockholders. **Noncumulative preferred stock** means dividends do not accumulate so that no past, unpaid dividends will be paid, unless the board of directors decides otherwise.

5. A corporation will sometimes buy back its own stock in the stock market. The shares held by the corporation are called **treasury stock** because they are physically held in the corporation's "treasury" where it keeps its cash and other certificates of value. Treasury Stock is a **contra-equity** account that reduces total shareholders' equity.

- The number of shares issued always equals the number of shares outstanding plus the number of shares in treasury. The number of shares outstanding is the number of shares

issued minus the number of shares in treasury.

- The **cost method** of recording a repurchase of treasury stock requires both assets (cash) and shareholders' equity (treasury stock) to be decreased by the cost to repurchase the stock. No gains or losses are to be recorded when a company purchases treasury stock or later resells it. If the stock is later reissued at a price that is more than this cost, the entry would be:

Assets	Liab.	Shareholders' equity	
		Contributed capital	**Retained earnings**
+ Cash		+ Treasury stock *(cost)* + Paid-in capital from treasury stock transactions *(price – cost)*	

If the price is less than cost, then additional paid-in capital would be reduced (instead of increased) by the difference between the cost and the price. If insufficient paid-in capital were available, then retained earnings would be reduced for the remaining amount.

- A corporation may buy back its own stock for several reasons. 1) to give employees stocks for bonuses or stock option plans; 2) to return excess cash to shareholders by buying back their shares or to use the excess cash to decrease the amount of equity compared to its debt; 3) to increase the company's earnings per share; 4) to reduce the cash needed to pay future dividends by decreasing the number of shares outstanding; or 5) to reduce chances of a hostile takeover.

6. A corporation may issue a **stock dividend** instead of a cash dividend. The stock dividend gives the shareholders more direct claim to equity by converting retained earnings to common stock (sometimes called capitalizing retained earnings). The effect of a stock dividend is:

Assets	Liab.	Shareholders' equity	
		Contributed capital	**Retained earnings**
		+ Common stock + Additional paid-in capital	- Retained earnings

A small stock dividend is a distribution of fewer than 25% of outstanding stocks and is recorded at the market value. Larger stock dividends are recorded at par value. A common stockholder's percentage ownership does not increase with a stock dividend because all the other common stockholders receive the same proportion.

7. A **stock split** occurs when a company increases the number of shares and proportionately decreases the par value. A 2-for-1 stock split means that the number of shares authorized, issued, and outstanding becomes two times the number before the split and the par value of a single share becomes one-half of the par value before the split. The market price of the stock should halve. However, financial experts believe the market prices decrease by less because of an increase in demand for the lower-priced stock, which has the effect of increasing the price. There is no effect of a stock split on the accounting equation or the corporation's financial position. The only change is the par value and the number of shares reported parenthetically in the shareholders' equity sections of the financial statements.

8. **Retained earnings,** known as earned capital (not contributed capital), is the net income minus dividends declared since the company began. It can be expressed as beginning retained earnings plus net income minus dividends and is typically shown in the statement of changes in shareholders' equity. Some corporations may show changes in retained earnings in a separate statement or at the bottom of the income statement.

9. **Initial public offering (IPO)** is the issuance of a corporation's stock to the public for the first time. In protecting investors, the Securities and Exchange Commission (SEC) requires the corporation to provide it with many reports, such as a prospectus that includes financial statements before "going public." Companies will go public to obtain significant contributed capital. The increase in shareholders' equity helps improve the capital structure (the amount of equity versus debt).

10. There are two ratios to help users analyze the shareholders' equity of a corporation. In general, the higher these ratios, the better.

- The **return on equity (ROE)** measures how profitable the company was in using the common stockholders' investment. ROE is calculated as net income (less preferred stock dividends) divided by the average common shareholders' equity.

- **Earnings per share (EPS)** is shown on the income statement and is a popular measure used to evaluate a company's performance and predict future stock prices. Basic or primary EPS is calculated as net income (less preferred stock dividends) divided by the weighted average number of common shares outstanding. The denominator should be a weighted average since shares may be issued or repurchased during the period. Another type of EPS is called diluted EPS and is calculated as if all convertible securities were converted into common stock. The effect is to dilute or reduce EPS because the larger number of shares in the denominator would make EPS smaller.

11. The risks associated with equity from an owner's point of view are the owner may lose money and the management of the company may not act in the best interest of the owner. To minimize the risk of loss, you should diversify your investments by buying stock in many different companies. Ideally, if a company or industry fails, the resulting loss would be offset by other stock doing well. The Sarbanes-Oxley Act of 2002 has addressed many of the risks of damage from unethical management. Controls that monitor the behavior and decisions of management – such as boards of directors and independent audits – will help minimize these risks.

Featured Exercise

Part A: Fill in the accounting equation below for the events of Tim's Ware, Inc. that occurred during 2009.

Tina's Ware, Inc.	Assets =	Liabilities +	Shareholders' equity	
			Contributed capital	Retained earnings
Beginning balances, January 1, 2009	Cash 500 Receivables (net) 6,000 Inventory 10,500 Prepaid insurance 600 Truck (net) 16,000	Accounts payable 5,000 Interest payable 700 Notes Payable 7,000	Common stock, $1 par value 10,000 Additional paid-in capital 5,000	Retained earnings 5,900
a	Received $6,000 by issuing 4,000 shares of its $1 par value common stock				
b	Purchased $20,000 of inventory on account				
c	Made sales of $40,000 on account; the cost of the sales was $30,000.				
d	Collected $44,000 of its receivables				
e	Paid $19,000 of amounts owed to suppliers				
f	Repurchased 200 shares of treasury stock for $400				
g	Paid $4,000 for payroll costs				
h	Adjusting entries are $200 for bad debts expense, $600 for insurance, $4,000 for depreciation, and $700 for interest owed				
i.	Sold 50 shares of treasury stock for $100				
j.	Declared a $3,000 dividend payable in 2010				

Part B: Using Part A, complete the statement of changes in shareholders' equity for Tim's Ware, Inc., for the year ended December 31, 2009.

Description	Common stock, $1 par value	Additional paid-in capital	Treasury stock	Retained earnings	Total
Tim's Ware, Inc. Statement of Changes in Shareholders' Equity For the Year Ended December 31, 2009					
December 31, 2008 balances					
Issued 4,000 shares of common stock for $6,000					
Repurchased 200 shares of treasury stock for $400					
Sold 50 shares of treasury stock for $100					
Declared a $3,000 dividend payable in 2010					
Net income					
Total					

Part C: Using Parts A and B, prepare the shareholders' equity section of the balance sheet at December 31, 2009. The number of shares authorized is 100,000 shares.

Part D: Answer the following questions using the information from Parts A, B, and C and assuming the average number of shares outstanding during 2009 is 13,900 shares.

1. How many shares of common stock are issued as of December 31, 2009?

2. How many shares of common stock are outstanding as of December 31, 2009?

3. What was the average selling price of a share of common stock?

4. Calculate the return on equity.

5. Calculate the earnings per share.

6. If Tim's Ware, Inc., did a 2-for-1 stock split, what would be the number of shares issued and what would be the par value of its common stock?

Solution

Part A: Fill in the accounting equation below for the events of Tim's Ware, Inc., that occurred during 2009.

Tina's Ware, Inc.	Assets =	Liabilities +	Shareholders' equity — Contributed capital	Shareholders' equity — Retained earnings
Beginning balances, January 1, 2009	Cash 500 Receivables (net) 6,000 Inventory 10,500 Prepaid insurance 600 Truck (net) 16,000	Accounts payable 5,000 Interest payable 700 Notes payable 7,000	Common stock, $1 par value 10,000 Additional paid-in capital 5,000	Retained earnings 5,900
a. Received $6,000 by issuing 4,000 shares of its $1 par value common stock	6,000 Cash		4,000 Common stock 2,000 Additional paid-in capital	
b. Purchased $20,000 of inventory on account	20,000 Inventory	20,000 Accounts payable		
c. Made sales of $40,000 on account; the cost of the sales was $30,000.	40,000 Receivables (30,000) Inventory			40,000 Sales (30,000) Cost of goods sold
d. Collected $44,000 of its receivables	44,000 Cash (44,000) Receivables			
e. Paid $19,000 of amounts owed to suppliers	(19,000) Cash	(19,000) Accounts payable		
f. Repurchased 200 shares of treasury stock for $400	(400) Cash		(400) Treasury stock	
g. Paid $4,000 for payroll costs	(4,000) Cash			(4,000) Payroll expense
h. Adjusting entries are $200 for bad debts expense, $600 for insurance, $4,000 for depreciation, and $700 for interest owed	(200) Allowance for uncollectible accounts (600) Prepaid insurance (4,000) Accumulated deprec.	700 Interest payable		(200) Bad debts expense (600) Insurance expense (4,000) Depreciation exp. (700) Interest expense
i. Sold 50 shares of treasury stock for $100	100 Cash		100 Treasury stock	
j. Declared a $3,000 dividend payable in 2010		3,000 Dividends payable		(3,000) Dividends

Part B:	Tim's Ware, Inc. Statement of Changes in Shareholders' Equity For the Year Ended December 31, 2009				
Description	Common stock, $1 par value	Additional paid-in capital	Treasury stock	Retained earnings	Total
December 31, 2008 balances	$10,000	$5,000	$0	$5,900	$20,900
Issued 4,000 shares of common stock for $6,000	4,000	2,000			6,000
Repurchased 200 shares of treasury stock for $400			(400)		(400)
Sold 50 shares of treasury stock for $100			100		100
Declared a $3,000 dividend payable in 2010				(3,000)	(3,000)
Net income				500	500
Total	$14,000	$7,000	$(300)	$3,400	$24,100

Part C:

December 31, 2009

Shareholders' equity
Common stock, par value $1 per share,
   authorized 100,000 shares, issued 14,000 shares $14,000
Additional paid-in capital   7,000
Treasury stock: 150 shares   (300)
Retained earnings   3,400
Total shareholders' equity $24,100

Part D:

1. Shares issued equals 14,000 shares.
2. Shares outstanding equals 13,850 (or 14,000 issued minus 150 treasury stock)
3. The average selling price equals $1.50 (or the sum of $14,000 common stock plus $7,000 additional paid-in capital divided by 14,000 shares of common stock issued).

4. Return on equity $= \dfrac{\text{net income}}{\text{average shareholders' equity}} = \dfrac{\$500}{(\$24,100 + \$20,900)/2} = 2.2\%$

5. Earnings per share $= \dfrac{\text{net income}}{\text{average shares outstanding}} = \dfrac{\$500}{13,900 \text{ shares}} = \$0.04$

6. The number of shares issued would be 28,000, or double the number of shares issued before the split. The par value of its common stock would be $0.50 or one half of the par value before the split.

Review Questions and Exercises

Completion Statements

Fill in the blank(s) to complete each statement.

1. The two sources of financing are debt financing (money from creditors), and _____ (money from owners).

2. Shareholders' equity is made up of _____ (owners' contributions) and _____ (earnings kept by the business).

3. When a corporation repurchases its own common stock, the shares are called _____. Since these shares reduce shareholders' equity, the account is called a _____-equity account.

4. The number of shares _____ always equals the number of shares _____ plus the number of shares in the _____.

5. Contributed capital (or paid-in capital) is divided into two parts: _____and _____.

6. The difference between the market price (the value received from the shareholder) and the par value is called _____ or _____.

7. The _____ date is the date the board of directors decides a dividend will be paid and a legal liability is created. Whoever owns the stock on the _____ date will receive the full dividend. The _____ date is when the cash is actually paid to the shareholders.

8. There are two types of preferred stock: _____ preferred stock, which means that dividends accumulate, and _____ preferred stock, which means dividends do not accumulate.

9. A _____ is the division of the current shares of stock by some factor to increase the number of shares and decrease the par value by the same factor.

10. The _____ measures how profitable the company was in using the common stockholders' investment and is calculated as net income (less preferred stock dividends) divided by the average common shareholders' equity.

True/False

Indicate whether each statement is true (T) or false (F).

_____1. The number of shares outstanding will always equal the number of shares issued minus the number of shares held as treasury stock.

_____2. The earnings per share is the amount of dividends the shareholder will receive.

_____3. The par value per share is the price the shareholders will pay when the shares are issued.

_____4. A reason a company will repurchase its own stock as treasury stock is to have shares it can later give to employees as part of a stock option plan.

_____5. Preferred stockholders do not have voting rights, but do have preference to dividends.

_____6. A stock dividend has the effect of reducing retained earnings and reducing cash.

_____7. Both stock dividends and stock splits increase the actual number of shares a shareholder will own, as well as increase the percentage of the shareholder's ownership.

_____8. The average selling price of common stock can be determined by dividing the sum of the balances in common stock and additional paid-in capital by the number of shares issued.

Multiple Choice

Select the best answer for each question.

_____1. The preferred stock dividend amount is calculated by:
A. dividing the total dividend by the number of shares of preferred stock plus common stock outstanding.
B. multiplying the dividend rate times the market price per share times the number of preferred stock shares outstanding.
C. multiplying the dividend rate times the par value per share times the number of preferred stock shares outstanding.
D. multiplying the total dividend times the percentage of preferred stock to common stock.

_____2. Diluted earnings per share (EPS) is reported on the income statement so that users can see what effect:
A. cumulative preferred stock dividends have on EPS.
B. contingent liabilities will have on EPS.
C. treasury stock has on EPS.
D. the convertible securities would have on EPS if they were converted into common stock.

_____3. Retained earnings is:
A. net income divided by the average number of shares outstanding.
B. the amount received in excess of par value.
C. the net income minus dividends since the inception of the company.
D. the minimum legal amount of earnings required to be kept by the company.

_____4. The par value of common stock represents the:
A. amount the stock sold for when it was originally issued.
B. legal minimum capital that must be retained in the company.
C. highest price a stock may be sold for.
D. amount of dividend the shareholder is to receive.

_____5. Stock that has dividends in arrears is called:
A. cumulative preferred stock.
B. convertible preferred stock.
C. cumulative common stock.
D. noncumulative preferred stock.

_____6. Aria's, Inc., has 1,000 shares of 5%, $100 par value cumulative preferred stock and 10,000 shares of $1 par value common stock outstanding. The company has not paid dividends in two years. In its third year, it paid the common stockholders a $2 per share dividend. How much did the preferred stockholders receive per share?

A. $100

B. $15

C. $6

D. $5

_____7. Aria's, Inc., has 1,000 shares of 5%, $100 par value cumulative preferred stock and 10,000 shares of $1 par value common stock. The company has not paid a dividend in two years. In its third year, it paid the common stockholders a $2 per share dividend. What was the total amount of dividends paid?

A. $35,000

B. $30,000

C. $20,000

D. $20,150

_____8. At the beginning of the year, the balance in retained earnings was $400,000. During the year, sales were $1,000,000, of which $800,000 was collected and expenses were $750,000, of which $400,000 had been paid. The company has outstanding 10,000 shares of 6%, $100 par value preferred stock and 100,000 shares of $0.10 par value common stock. The dividend paid to the common stockholders was $1 per share. Calculate the ending retained earnings.

A. $490,000

B. $410,000

C. $240,000

D. $ 90,000

_____9. Mr. Cello bought 4,000 shares of Ventures, Inc., $1 par value common stock directly from Ventures, Inc. for $80,000. Mr. Cello sold 1,000 of his shares to Mr. Bilo for $30,000. The result for Ventures, Inc. will be:

A. shareholders' equity will decrease by $80,000.

B. net income will increase by $10,000 from the gain on the sale of common stock.

C. Shareholders' equity will be unaffected by the sale.

D. Both A and B above are correct.

_____10. A company has treasury stock that cost $50,000. If it resells this stock for $40,000, then:

A. additional paid-in capital is reduced by $10,000.

B. additional paid-in capital is reduced by $50,000.

C. treasury stock is increased by $40,000.

D. shareholders' equity is increased by $50,000.

Exercises

1. For each event listed below, fill in the correct dollar amounts in the appropriate box(es) to show the effect of the event on shareholders' equity accounts.

Business event	6%, $100 par value preferred stock	$1 par value common stock	Additional paid-in capital	Retained earnings	Treasury stock
January 1, 2009 beginning balances	$50,000	$100,000	$300,000	$400,000	$(10,000)
Sold 10,000 additional shares of $1 par value common stock for $4 per share					
Purchased 1,000 shares of its own stock for $5,000					
Net income for the year was $50,000					
Declared dividends of $10,000					
December 31, 2009 ending balances					

2. For each of the transactions below, show the effect on the accounting equation by circling one item in each column.

a. On January 1, 2009, Ventures, Inc., declared a $50,000 dividend. The date of record is January 31, 2009 and the date of payment is February 15, 2009.

Total assets	Total liabilities	Total shareholders' equity	
		Contributed capital	Retained earnings
Increase	Increase	Increase	Increase
Decrease	Decrease	Decrease	Decrease
No effect	No effect	No effect	No effect

b. On January 31, 2009, Ventures, Inc., updated its stock records.

Total assets	Total liabilities	Total shareholders' equity	
		Contributed capital	Retained earnings
Increase	Increase	Increase	Increase
Decrease	Decrease	Decrease	Decrease
No effect	No effect	No effect	No effect

c. On February 15, 2009, Ventures, Inc., paid the $50,000 dividend in a. above.

Total assets	Total liabilities	Total shareholders' equity	
		Contributed capital	Retained earnings
Increase	Increase	Increase	Increase
Decrease	Decrease	Decrease	Decrease
No effect	No effect	No effect	No effect

d. On February 28, 2009, Ventures, Inc., repurchased $5,000 of its own stock.

Total assets	Total liabilities	Total shareholders' equity
		Contributed capital +Retained earnings
Increase	Increase	Increase
Decrease	Decrease	Decrease
No effect	No effect	No effect

e. On March 31, 2009, Ventures, Inc., paid a $10,000 stock dividend.

Total assets	Total liabilities	Total shareholders' equity	
		Contributed capital	Retained earnings
Increase	Increase	Increase	Increase
Decrease	Decrease	Decrease	Decrease
No effect	No effect	No effect	No effect

f. On May 31, 2009, Ventures, Inc., split its stock 2 for 1.

Total assets	Total liabilities	Total shareholders' equity	
		Contributed capital	Retained earnings
Increase	Increase	Increase	Increase
Decrease	Decrease	Decrease	Decrease
No effect	No effect	No effect	No effect

3. Capital Venture, Inc., began operations in January 2009 by issuing common stock for $10 per share. Net income for 2009 was $500,000 and dividends of $100,000 were declared. Fill in the missing amounts in the spaces provided.

	December 31, 2009
6% preferred stock, $50 par value, 500 shares authorized and issued	(a)
Common stock, $1 par value, 8,000,000 shares authorized, (b)_____ shares issued	$900,000
Additional paid-in capital in excess of par	(c)
Retained earnings	(d)
Treasury stock (1,000 shares at cost)	(25,000)
Total shareholders' equity	(e)

(f) How many shares are outstanding as of December 31, 2009?

4. Tim's Ware's had an initial public offering and sold 200,000 shares of $2 par value common stock for a total of $3,000,000.

a	What was the average selling price for each share of stock?	
b	What amount should be reported for the Common stock?	
c	What amount should be reported for the Additional paid-in capital?	

Solutions to Review Questions and Exercises

Completion Statements

1. equity financing
2. contributed capital, retained earnings
3. treasury stock, contra
4. issued, outstanding, treasury
5. paid-in capital, retained earnings
6. paid-in capital in excess of par, additional paid-in capital
7. declaration, record, payment
8. cumulative, noncumulative
9. stock split
10. return on equity

True/False

1. True
2. False   EPS is a company's net income (not dividends), less preferred stock dividends if any, on a per share basis.
3. False   The par value represents the maximum responsibility of a shareholder and does not have any relationship to the market price of that share.
4. True
5. True
6. False   A stock dividend's effect on the accounting equation is to reduce retained earnings and increase common stock. A cash (not stock) dividend reduces cash when it is paid.

7. False   Both stock dividends and splits increase the number of shares a shareholder will own. However, since all shareholders receive the same proportion of stock, their ownership percentage remains the same.

8. True

Multiple Choice

1. C   Preferred stock typically has a dividend rate and par value stated on the certificate. The preferred stock dividend is the dividend rate times the par value. Common stock does not have a dividend rate and will receive the dividends that are remaining only after the preferred stockholders' dividends have been met.

2. D   The diluted EPS assumes that all of the company's convertible securities have been converted into common stock. This makes the denominator larger, causing the EPS to be smaller or diluted.

3. C   Retained earnings equals beginning retained earnings plus net income minus dividends.

4. B   The par value has no relevance to the market price. Most companies' par value is set well below the selling price of the stock. The lower the par value the less likely a company's equity will fall below this legal minimum capital that must be retained in the company.

5. A   Only cumulative preferred stockholders have the right to receive past, unpaid dividends before other shareholders receive any dividends.

6. B   The preferred dividend per share is $5 which equals the dividend rate, 5%, times the par value of $100. Since the stock is cumulative, the dividend will equal $15 per share (3 years x $5).

7. A   The cumulative preferred shareholders receive $15 per share. The total dividends paid is $35,000, which equals $15,000 to preferred shareholders (or $15 per share times 1,000 shares) plus $20,000 to common shareholders (or $2 per common share times 10,000 shares).

8. A   Beginning retained earnings of $400,000 plus net income of $250,000 (or $1,000,000 minus $750,000) minus dividends of $160,000 (6% times $100 par value times 10,000 preferred shares plus $1 times 100,000 common shares) equals ending retained earnings of $490,000.

9. C   When the company issued 4,000 shares to Mr. Cello, its contributed capital increased by $80,000. When Mr. Cello sells his shares to another party, there is no effect on Ventures' shareholders' equity.

10. A   The reissuance of treasury stock at an amount below cost causes cash to increase by $40,000 and treasury stock to increase by $50,000. Additional paid-in capital is decreased by $10,000 to balance the accounting equation.

Exercises

1. Business event	6%, $100 par value preferred stock	$1 par value common stock	Additional paid-in capital	Retained earnings	Treasury stock
January 1, 2009 beginning balances	$50,000	$100,000	$300,000	$400,000	$(10,000)
Sold 10,000 additional shares of $1 par value common stock for $4 per share		10,000 *$1 x 10,000*	30,000 *($4 – 1) x 10,000*		
Purchased 1,000 shares of its own stock for $5,000					(5,000)
Net income for the year was $50,000				50,000	
Declared dividends of $10,000				(10,000)	
December 31, 2009 ending balances	$50,000	$110,000	$330,000	$440,000	$(15,000)

2.	Total assets	Total liabilities	Total shareholders' equity	
			Contributed capital	**Retained earnings**
a	No effect	Increased	No effect	Decreased
b	No effect	No effect	No effect	No effect
c	Decrease	Decrease	No effect	No effect
d	Decrease	No effect	Decrease	
e	No effect	No effect	Increase	Decrease
f	No effect	No effect	No effect	No effect

3.	**December 31, 2009**
6% preferred stock, $50 par value, 500 shares authorized and issued	(a) $25,000 *$50 par value x 500 shares*
Common stock, $1 par value, 8,000,000 shares authorized, (b) 900,000 shares issued *($900,000/$1 par value)*	$900,000
Additional paid-in capital in excess of par	(c) $8,100,000 *($10 - 1) x 900,000 shares*
Retained earnings	(d) $400,000 *$500,000 – 100,000*
Treasury stock (1,000 shares at cost)	(25,000)
Total shareholders' equity	(e) $9,400,000

(f) 900,000 shares issued minus 1,000 treasury shares equals 899,000 shares outstanding.

4.

a	What was the average selling price for each share of stock?	$15 *$3,000,000/200,000 shares*
b	What amount should be reported for the common stock?	$400,000 *$2 x 200,000 shares*
c	What amount should be reported for the additional paid-in capital?	$2,600,000 *($15 - $2) x 200,000 shares*

CHAPTER 9
PREPARING AND ANALYZING THE STATEMENT OF CASH FLOWS

Chapter Overview

The statement of cash flows, which describes in detail all of a company's cash receipts and cash payments, is one of the financial statements required by GAAP. In this chapter you will learn to prepare the three sections of the statement of cash flows: 1) cash from operating activities, which may be prepared using either the direct or the indirect method; 2) cash from investing activities; and 3) cash from financing activities. In learning to prepare the statement of cash flows, you should gain a clearer understanding of the difference between accrual accounting and cash-basis accounting.

Chapter Highlights

1. Cash is a very important asset. Many companies go bankrupt each year because they do not have enough cash at the right time to pay their bills. A cash budget is useful for estimating in advance the cash inflows and outflows that a company expects. If a company expects a shortfall, it can plan ahead of time and secure a line of credit, borrow the money needed, or change the timing of expected cash receipts and payments. At the end of the accounting period, managers can use this same budget to evaluate performance by comparing it with actual events. This year's cash budget is also useful for planning next year's cash activity.

2. GAAP allows two ways of preparing the cash from operating activities section of the statement of cash flows: the **direct method** and the **indirect method**. With the direct method, cash inflows and outflows are shown directly. With the indirect method, the statement begins with net income, an accrual-based number, and adjusts it to cash from operating activities. Regardless of the method used, net cash flow from operating activities should be the same dollar amount. The other two sections, cash from investing activities and cash from financing activities, are prepared in the same way for both the direct and indirect methods.

3. The first section of the statement of cash flows shows cash from operating activities, where the cash inflows and cash outflows from the normal, day-to-day activities are reported. Typical operating cash inflows are:
- Cash collected from customers
- Cash collected for interest

Typical operating cash outflows are:
- Cash paid to employees
- Cash paid to suppliers for inventory
- Cash paid for operating expenses
- Cash paid for interest
- Cash paid for taxes

4. The second section of the statement of cash flows is the investing section, also known as **cash from investing activities**, where the cash inflows and cash outflows for long-term business assets and for investments are reported. Typical investing cash inflows are:
- Cash received from the sale of property, plant, and equipment
- Cash from the sale of marketable securities
- Cash received when amounts loaned to others are repaid

Typical investing cash outflows are:
- Cash paid to buy property, plant, and equipment
- Cash paid for investments
- Cash loaned to others

5. The third section of the statement of cash flows is the financing section, also known as **cash from financing activities**, where the cash inflows and cash outflows for the principal on loans, contributions from owners, and payments to owners are reported. Typical financing cash inflows are:
- Cash received from the sale of stock
- Cash received from borrowing

Typical financing cash outflows are:
- Cash paid for treasury stock
- Cash paid to retire debt principal
- Cash paid for dividends

6. Most companies keep their accounting records on an accrual basis so that they can easily prepare financial statements in accordance with GAAP. If a company sells goods on account, it will recognize sales revenue for goods that have been sold even if cash has not yet been received. Uncollected accounts receivable represent revenue that has been earned but has not been collected in cash. Moreover, the company may have collected cash during the accounting period from sales on account recorded in a previous accounting period. For both of these reasons, the amount of cash received during an accounting period will not necessarily be the same as the revenue earned during that period.

To convert the accrual-basis sales revenue found on the income statement to cash collected from customers for the statement of cash flows, you must analyze the change in accounts receivable during the accounting period by looking at balance sheets for the beginning and end of the period. If accounts receivable increased during the period, then some of the current period's sales have not yet been collected from customers. This increase in accounts receivable should be subtracted from sales revenue to determine the amount of cash collected.

Every revenue or expense reported on the accrual-basis income statement may be different from the amount of cash actually received or paid. Each income statement line item must be examined along with changes in the related current asset or current liability accounts to determine the amount of cash actually received or paid. For example, a company might show salary expense of $30,000 on its income statement. This represents the cost of services provided by employees during the accounting period, regardless of whether these employees have been paid in cash or not. If the related current liability account, salaries payable, also decreased $400 during the period, then the company must have paid cash for more than just the $30,000 current period's expense. The

decrease in salaries payable should be added to the $30,000 salary expense to determine the amount of cash paid to employees.

7. There are two possible ways to prepare the cash from operating activities section of the statement of cash flows. The direct method begins with the income statement. Each revenue and expense must be analyzed to determine the amount of cash received or paid. In your textbook, see Tom's Wear's third month of business – March – to see how to convert revenues to cash collected and expenses to cash paid.

- Tom's Wear's income statement shows sales revenue of $2,000 for the month ended March 31. During the month, accounts receivable grew from $150 at the beginning of the month to $2,000 at the end of the month, an increase of $1,850. This means that none of March's $2,000 in sales revenue has been received in cash yet. Cash collected from customers must be $2,000 in sales revenue minus the $1,850 increase in accounts receivable, or $150.

- Tom's Wear's income statement shows cost of goods sold of $800 for the same month. The first step in calculating cash paid for inventory is to determine how much inventory was purchased during March. Inventory grew from $100 at the beginning of the month to $300 at the end of the month, an increase of $200. Tom's Wear must have purchased enough inventory to cover the $800 in cost of goods sold and to increase its inventory by $200 as well, a total of $1,000 in inventory purchased. However, this does not tell us how much cash the company actually paid for inventory, since often inventory is purchased on account, not for cash. We must also look at changes in accounts payable for the period. Accounts payable went from $800 at the beginning of the month to $0 at the end of the month, a decrease of $800. The company must have paid the full $1,000 for March's purchases plus another $800 for inventory purchased in a previous period, a total of $1,800 cash paid for inventory in March.

- The March income statement for Tom's Wear shows depreciation expense of $100. This represents part of the historical cost of equipment allocated to expense for the current accounting period. No cash is ever paid for depreciation expense.

- The company's income statement shows insurance expense of $50 for the month. During the month, the balance in prepaid insurance went from $125 at the beginning of the month to $75 at the end of the month, a decrease of $50. Clearly, the $50 in March insurance expense came from a policy purchased in a previous month, not from a current cash payment. No cash was paid for insurance in March.

- Finally, Tom's Wear's income statement shows interest expense of $30. During March, the balance in interest payable increased from $0 at the beginning of the month to $30 at the end of the month. The company owes the entire $30 in interest. No cash was paid for interest during the month.

- Although we have covered all of the line items on the income statement, we must look at the balance sheet to make sure that all changes in current assets and current liabilities have been included. Property, plant, and equipment, represented by the $3,900 in the machine account, is not a current asset, so it does not affect cash from operating activities. Among the current liabilities, other payables decreased from $50 at the beginning of the month to $0 at the end of the month. Although no other operating expenses appear on the income statement, the company must have paid $50 for other expenses reported during a previous accounting period. Notes payable is a long-term liability, not a current liability, so it does not affect cash from operating activities.

The cash from operating activities section for Tom's Wear's statement of cash flows, prepared using the direct method, looks like this:

Cash from operating activities:

Cash from customers	$ 150
Cash paid to vendors	(1,800)
Cash paid for other expenses	(50)
Net increase (decrease) in cash from operating activities	$(1,700)

8. The Financial Accounting Standards Board (FASB) prefers that companies use the direct method to prepare the operating activities section of the statement of cash flows. However, the FASB requires that companies using the direct method must also provide a reconciliation of net income and cash from operating activities, which is essentially the same as using the indirect method. Most companies, then, use the indirect method to report cash flows from operating activities.

Using the indirect method, the operating activities section begins with net income. Any amounts that affect net income but do not affect cash are removed. Then changes in each current asset and current liability account are analyzed to determine the effect on cash. Tom's Wear's income statement shows net income of $1,020. To this amount, add $100 in depreciation expense because this expense decreases income but does not decrease cash.

- Accounts receivable grew from $150 at the beginning of the month to $2,000 at the end of the month, an increase of $1,850. If accounts receivable increase, it means that sales revenue has not been collected in cash. This $1,850 increase in accounts receivable should be subtracted for the calculation of cash from operating activities.

- Inventory increased from $100 at the beginning of March to $300 at the end of March. This $200 increase in a current asset represents an inventory purchase that might have been paid for in cash, and should be subtracted because it potentially decreases the cash provided by operating activities.

- Prepaid insurance went from $125 at the beginning of the month to $75 at the end of the month, a decrease of $50. This decrease in a current asset represents an expense on the income statement that decreased income without requiring a decrease in cash as well. The $50 should be added to net income in calculating cash from operating activities.

- Prepaid rent was $0 at the beginning of March and $0 at the end of March, too. Since it did not change, it did not affect either income or cash for the month, and it can be ignored.

- The change in the machine account, a long-term asset, does not affect cash from operating activities because buying and selling property, plant, and equipment is an investing activity, not an operating activity.

- Accounts payable went from $800 at the beginning of March to $0 at the end of March. This decrease in a current liability represents cash paid out by Tom's Wear, and a decrease in cash provided by operating activities. Similarly, the $50 decrease in other payables decreases the cash provided by operating activities.

- Interest payable increased from $0 at the beginning of the period to $30 at the end of the period. This means that the $30 expense, which decreased net income on the income statement, did not decrease cash because the company did not pay anything for interest in March. This decrease in a current liability should be added to net income in calculating cash from operating activities.

- Notes payable is a long-term liability, not a current liability. Increases and decreases in long-term debt are financing, not operating, activities.

The cash from operating activities section for Tom's Wear's statement of cash flows, prepared using the indirect method, looks like this:

Net income		$ 1,020
+	Depreciation expense	100
-	Increase in accounts receivable	(1,850)
-	Increase in inventory	(200)
+	Decrease in prepaid insurance	50
-	Decrease in payables	
	(- 800 – 50 + 30)	(820)
Net cash from operating activities		$(1,700)

Notice that cash from operating activities is the same $(1,700) under both the direct and indirect methods.

9. The format of the cash from investing activities section is the same, whether the operating activities are presented under the direct method or indirect method. Analyze changes in noncurrent assets to determine cash received or paid for investing activities.

- In the month of March, the balance in Tom's Wear's machine account increased from $0 to $3,900, net of $100 accumulated depreciation. The original cost of the machine must have been $4,000. Since long-term assets are often expensive, it is possible that this entire amount was not paid in cash and we must look further in the company's records. Tom's Wear paid $1,000 in cash and signed a note for the $3,000 remainder. Only the cash paid will appear in the investing activities section of the statement, but the $3,000 note will be shown in a footnote so that the statement includes all major investing activities, even those that did not involve cash.

10. Similarly, the format of the cash from financing activities section is the same, whether the operating activities are presented under the direct method or indirect method. Analyze changes in noncurrent liabilities and owners' equity accounts for evidence of financing activities.

- Notes payable increased from $0 at the beginning of March to $3,000 at the end of March. Tom's Wear did not receive cash for the note payable, but instead used it to finance the purchase of equipment. Since no cash was received, the note will not be reported in the financing activities section of the statement, but will be described in a footnote.

- There was no change in Tom's Wear's Common stock account during March. Apparently, no cash was received from the sale of stock. Retained earnings went from $1,220 to $2,240 during the month, an increase of $1,020. Since this increase is exactly equal to net income, no dividends were declared or paid.

The investing and financing activities sections of Tom's Wear's statement of cash flows will look like this:

Cash from investing activities:

Purchase of machine*	(1,000)
Net cash from investing activities	(1,000)

Cash from financing activities: 0

* A $4,000 machine was purchased for $1,000 cash and a $3,000 note payable.

11. GAAP requires companies that use the indirect method to disclose cash paid for interest and taxes somewhere in the financial statements.

12. Investors hope to see a positive cash flow from operating activities. In the long run, a company must generate positive operating cash flow or it will not survive. The investing activities section of the statement of cash flows shows the company's plans. Negative investing cash flow means the company has invested in long-term assets, which may indicate expansion, or at least replacement of aging productive assets. Failure to invest in property, plant and equipment may mean the company has a problem. The financing activities section shows how the company is financed, with debt or with equity.

Financial analysts sometimes calculate **free cash flow**, which is cash flow from operating activities minus cash paid for dividends and capital expenditures. This is used as a measure of a company's ability to make future investments.

13. Investors' risk associated with the statement of cash flows includes managements' misclassification of cash inflows and outflows. Analysts interpret positive net cash from operating activities as a signal for positive future growth. Thus, management may be pressured into acting unethically and misclassifying cash inflows from investing or financing activities as cash inflows from operating activities. Management could also create positive cash from operating activities by misclassifying operating cash outflows as investing or financing activities.

Featured Exercise

Megabucks, Inc.
Income Statement
For the Year Ended December 31, 2009

Sales revenue		$2,000,000
Expenses		
Cost of goods sold	$1,080,000	
Salary expense	572,000	
Depreciation expense	24,000	
Other operating expenses	138,000	
Interest expense	38,800	1,852,800
Net income		$ 147,200

Megabucks, Inc.
Comparative Balance Sheets
At December 31, 2009 and 2008

	2009	2008	Increase (Decrease)
Cash	$ 120,800	$ 40,800	$ 80,000
Accounts receivable	84,000	132,000	(48,000)
Inventory	408,000	384,000	24,000
Equipment (net of depreciation)	480,000	504,000	(24,000)
Total	$1,092,800	$1,060,800	
Accounts payable	$ 98,400	$ 63,200	$ 35,200
Salaries payable	7,600	16,000	(8,400)
Interest payable	9,600	21,600	(12,000)
Bonds payable	400,000	400,000	0
Common stock	104,000	104,000	0
Retained earnings*	473,200	456,000	17,200
Total	$1,092,800	$1,060,800	

*During 2009, Megabucks declared and paid a cash dividend of $130,000.

Part A: Prepare a statement of cash flows for the year ended December 31, 2009, using the direct method.

Megabucks, Inc.
Statement of Cash Flows
For the Year Ended December 31, 2009

Part B: Prepare a statement of cash flows for the year ended December 31, 2009, using the indirect method.

Megabucks, Inc.
Statement of Cash Flows
For the Year Ended December 31, 2009

Solution

Part A

Megabucks, Inc.
Statement of Cash Flows
For the Year Ended December 31, 2009

Cash from operating activities

Cash from customers	$ 2,048,000	
Cash paid to vendors	(1,068,800)	
Cash paid for salaries	(580,400)	
Cash paid for other operating expenses	(138,000)	
Cash paid for interest	(50,800)	
Net cash from operating activities		$ 210,000

Cash from investing activities		0

Cash from financing activities

Cash paid for dividends	(130,000)	
Net cash from financing activities		(130,000)

Net increase (decrease) in cash		$ 80,000

Part B

Megabucks, Inc.
Statement of Cash Flows
For the Year Ended December 31, 2009

Cash from operating activities

Net income	$147,200	
+ Depreciation expense	24,000	
+ Decrease in Accounts receivable	48,000	
- Increase in Inventory	(24,000)	
+ Increase in Accounts payable	35,200	
- Decrease in Salaries payable	(8,400)	
- Decrease in Interest payable	(12,000)	
Net cash from operating activities		$210,000

Cash from investing activities		0

Cash from financing activities

Cash paid for dividends	(130,000)	
Net cash from financing activities		(130,000)

Net increase (decrease) in cash		$ 80,000

Review Questions and Exercises

Completion Statements

Fill in the blank(s) to complete each statement.

1. The first section of the statement of cash flows is _____.

2. The second section of the statement of cash flows is _____.

3. The third section of the statement of cash flows is _____.

4. There are two ways to present cash flows from operating activities: the _____ method and the _____ method.

5. Companies that use the direct method of calculating cash from operating activities must also provide a_____.

6. Companies that use the indirect method of calculating cash from operating activities must also report cash paid for _____ and cash paid for _____ somewhere in their financial statements.

7. Investors hope to see _____ cash flow from operating activities.

8. Investors look at cash used by _____for evidence of expansion.

9. The cash from _____ section shows how a company finances its assets.

10. A _____ is a detailed plan of a company's estimated cash receipts and disbursements.

True/False

Indicate whether each statement is true (T) or false (F).

_____ 1. The Financial Accounting Standards Board prefers that companies use the direct method of reporting cash from operating activities.

_____ 2. Most companies use the direct method of reporting cash from operating activities.

_____ 3. Depreciation expense decreases a company's cash.

_____ 4. A company that uses the direct method will show more cash from operating activities than a company that uses the indirect method.

_____ 5. There are two acceptable ways to report cash from investing activities: the direct method and the indirect method.

_____ 6. Only new companies need to prepare a cash budget to obtain financing.

_____ 7. Negative cash flow from investing activities is usually good.

_____ 8.   If a company issues a five-year note payable to buy equipment, the note will not appear on the statement of cash flows because it does not involve receipt or payment of cash.

_____ 9.   Only the largest companies are required to prepare a statement of cash flows.

_____ 10.   If a company uses the indirect method of calculating cash from operating activities, its statement of cash flows begins with net income.

Multiple Choice

_____ 1.   In the long run, a company must generate positive cash flow from _____ or it will not survive.
A. operating activities
B. investing activities
C. financing activities
D. operating, investing, or financing activities

_____ 2.   Which of the following financial statements explains why a company's cash balance changed over a period of time?
A. Income statement
B. Balance sheet
C. Statement of cash flows
D. Both B. and C. are correct.

Use the following information to answer the next three questions:
Our Feathered Friends, Inc., reported credit sales of $1,500,000 for 2009. Cost of goods sold was $700,000. The following additional information is available from the company's records:

	December 31, 2009	December 31, 2008
Accounts receivable	$50,000	$40,000
Inventory	75,000	80,000
Accounts payable	30,000	25,000

_____ 3.   How much cash did the company collect from customers in 2009?
A. $1,500,000
B. $1,510,000
C. $1,490,000
D. $10,000

_____ 4.   How much inventory did the company buy from vendors in 2009?
A. $700,000
B. $5,000
C. $705,000
D. $695,000

_____ 5. How much cash was paid to vendors in 2009?
   A. $690,000
   B. $695,000
   C. $700,000
   D. $705,000

Use the following information to answer the next two questions. Both of these companies are merchandisers that began operations this year.

	X Company	Y Company
Cash from operating activities	$ 20,000	$ 60,000
Cash from investing activities	(200,000)	(100,000)
Cash from financing activities	230,000	90,000
Net increase in cash	$ 50,000	$ 50,000

_____ 6. Which of these two companies appears to have made the larger purchases of property, plant, and equipment during the year?
   A. X Company
   B. Y Company
   C. Both companies have made the same purchases.
   D. Neither company has made any purchases.

_____ 7. Which of these two companies is likely to pay the larger cash dividend per share of stock next month?
   A. X Company
   B. Y Company
   C. They will pay the same amount.
   D. The answer cannot be determined from the information given.

_____ 8. Oblique, Inc., prepares its statement of cash flows using the indirect method. In calculating cash from operating activities, increases in current assets other than cash should be:
   A. added to net income.
   B. subtracted from net income.
   C. ignored.
   D. multiplied by net income.

_____ 9. Oblique, Inc., prepares its statement of cash flows using the indirect method. In calculating cash from operating activities, increases in current liabilities should be:
   A. added to net income.
   B. subtracted from net income.
   C. ignored.
   D. multiplied by net income.

_____ 10. Cash flows from investing activities can be discovered by analyzing changes in a company's:
   A. current asset accounts.
   B. current liability accounts.
   C. long-term asset accounts.
   D. long-term liabilities and shareholders' equity accounts.

Exercises

1. Put an X in the appropriate box to identify each of these activities as operating, investing, or financing.

	Activity	Operating	Investing	Financing
a	Cash paid to purchase treasury stock			
b	Cash received for interest			
c	Cash paid to buy machinery			
d	Cash paid to employees			
e	Cash paid for stock of other companies			
f	Cash received from the sale of the company's own stock			
g	Cash paid for interest			
h	Cash paid for dividends			
i	Cash paid for taxes			
j	Cash received from customers			
k	Cash received on loans previously made to other companies			
l	Cash received from selling equipment			
m	Cash paid for rent on warehouse			
n	Cash paid to retire the principal on debt			
o	Cash collected on accounts receivable			
p	Cash received from selling investments in stock of other companies			
q	Cash paid to buy land that will be used for the company's new store			
r	Cash paid for utilities used in one of the company's stores			
s	Cash paid for inventory			
t	Cash received from borrowing			
u	Cash loaned to other companies			

2. The column below on the left lists line items from the income statement. The column on the right lists current assets and current liabilities. Match each income statement item with the related balance sheet account(s) used for preparing the statement of cash flows.

_____ 1. Sales

_____ 2. Salary expense

_____ 3. Cost of goods sold

_____ 4. Interest expense

_____ 5 Interest revenue

_____ 6. Insurance expense

_____ 7. Operating expenses

_____ 8. Rent expense

A. Interest payable

B. Other payables

C. Inventory and Accounts payable

D. Interest receivable

E. Salaries payable

F. Accounts receivable

G. Prepaid rent

H. Prepaid insurance

3. Use the information below to prepare the cash flows from investing activities and cash flows from financing activities sections of the statement of cash flows. Some of the items listed are not investing or financing activities.

   a. Sold equipment for $6,000 cash that had a book value of $8,000

   b. Paid $50,000 cash to retire bonds payable

   c. Bought an $80,000 building by making an $8,000 cash down payment and signing a 20-year mortgage note for the remainder

   d. Made a $4,000 payment on an installment note; $600 of this payment was interest and the rest was principal

   e. Issued 5,000 shares of $1 par value common stock for $20 per share

   f. The company had 500 shares of treasury stock that cost $8,000. It sold these shares for $10,000.

   g. Declared and paid a cash dividend of $40,000

   h. Paid $12,000 for the bonds of another company to be held as a long-term investment

   i. Received $1,000 interest from the investment in bonds of another company

4. Describe two unethical ways management could misclassify cash inflows and outflows to appear more favorable to analysts.

Solutions to Review Questions and Exercises

Completion Statements
1. cash from operating activities
2. cash from investing activities
3. cash from financing activities
4. direct, indirect
5. reconciliation of net income and cash from operating activities
6. interest, income taxes
7. positive
8. investing activities
9. financing activities
10. cash budget

True/False

1. True
2. False Around 90% of companies use the indirect method.
3. False The entry to record depreciation expense decreases the book value of the asset and decreases owners' equity. Cash is never paid for depreciation expense.
4. False Cash from operating activities should be the same regardless of the method used.
5. False There is only one acceptable way to report cash from investing activities. There are two acceptable ways to report cash from operating activities.
6. False Lenders expect to see a cash budget from all borrowers.
7. True
8. False Noncash investing and financing activities are described in footnotes to the statement of cash flows, so that the statement summarizes all important investing and financing activities.
9. False The statement of cash flows is one of the financial statements required by GAAP.
10. True

Multiple Choice

1. A In the long run, a business must be able to generate enough cash from normal, day-to-day activities to pay for its operations, investments in long-term assets, loans from creditors, and dividends to owners. In the short run, a company can raise cash by borrowing or by selling stock. However, if it cannot generate a positive cash flow from operating activities to pay back the loans, eventually creditors will be unwilling to lend the company any more money. Similarly, it will become very difficult to raise additional cash by issuing more shares of stock, since investors will be unwilling to buy more shares.

2. C A. is wrong because the income statement shows revenues earned and expenses incurred, not cash received and cash paid. B. is wrong because the balance sheet shows the cash balance at a single point in time, not the detailed changes in cash during the accounting period. Only the statement of cash flows shows the inflows and outflows of cash during an accounting period.

3. C The $10,000 increase in accounts receivable ($50,000 – 40,000) means that some customers who purchased merchandise on account in 2009 have not yet paid the company. Credit sales of $1,500,000 minus the $10,000 increase in accounts receivable equals $1,490,000. Or,
   $40,000 beginning A/R, plus $1,500,000 in additional A/R from sales during the year, minus $50,000 ending A/R equals $1,490,000.

4. D The $5,000 decrease in inventory ($75,000 – 80,000) means that some of the merchandise sold came from beginning inventory. Cost of goods sold of $700,000, minus the $5,000 decrease in inventory, equals $695,000. Or $700,000 in cost of goods sold, plus $75,000 in ending inventory, means that the company had $775,000 of merchandise available for sale during the year. If

$80,000 of this merchandise came from beginning inventory, the remaining $695,000 must have been purchased during the year. ($700,000 +75,000 – 80,000 = $695,000)

5. A The $5,000 increase in accounts payable ($30,000 – 25,000) means that the company did not pay for all of the inventory it purchased in 2009. Purchases of $695,000, minus the $5,000 increase in accounts payable, equals $690,000. Or, beginning accounts payable of $25,000, plus $695,000 in additional accounts payable during the year, minus $30,000 in ending accounts payable, equals $690,000 paid in cash.

6. A Company X has paid more cash for investing activities. Purchases of property, plant, and equipment are investing activities.

7. B Y Company has generated more cash from operating activities than X Company and is in a better position for paying dividends. In addition, Y Company, with less cash coming in from financing activities, probably has less debt, so it does not need to worry as much about cash for future interest payments. Furthermore, less cash from financing activities probably means that Y Company issued fewer shares of stock than X Company. Each share of Y Company stock can receive a larger cash dividend without requiring as much total cash as X Company would need for the same dividend per share.

8. B Increases in current assets such as inventory or prepaid rent represent purchases of goods or services that might have required a payment of cash. An increase in the current asset accounts receivable means that some of the current period's sales have not been collected in cash yet.

9. A Increases in current liabilities such as accounts payable or salaries payable represent purchases of goods or services that were not paid for in cash. They are associated with expenses that decreased net income, but did not decrease cash.

10. C Typical investing activities are purchases or sales of stock in another company or property, plant, and equipment. These are long-term assets. A. and B. are wrong because changes in current assets and current liabilities are used to analyze cash from operating activities. D. is wrong because changes in long-term liabilities and shareholders' equity accounts are indicators of financing activities.

Exercises

1.	Activity	Operating	Investing	Financing
a	Cash paid to purchase treasury stock			X
b	Cash received for interest	X		
c	Cash paid to buy machinery		X	
d	Cash paid to employees	X		
e	Cash paid for stock of other companies		X	
f	Cash received from the sale of the company's own stock			X
g	Cash paid for interest	X		
h	Cash paid for dividends			X
i	Cash paid for taxes	X		
j	Cash received from customers	X		
k	Cash received on loans previously made to other companies		X	
l	Cash received from selling equipment		X	
m	Cash paid for rent on warehouse	X		
n	Cash paid to retire the principal on debt			X
o	Cash collected on accounts receivable	X		
p	Cash received from selling investments in stock		X	
q	Cash paid to buy land		X	
r	Cash paid for utilities used in one of the company's stores	X		
s	Cash paid for inventory	X		
t	Cash received from borrowing			X
u	Cash loaned to other companies		X	

2.

F 1. Sales/ Accounts receivable
E 2. Salary expense/ Salaries payable
C 3. Cost of goods sold/ Inventory and Accounts payable
A 4. Interest expense/ Interest payable
D 5   Interest revenue/ Interest receivable
H 6. Insurance expense/ Prepaid insurance
B 7. Operating expenses/ Other payables
G 8. Rent expense/ Prepaid rent

3.

Cash from investing activities

Sale of equipment	$ 6,000	
Purchase of building*	(8,000)	
Purchased bonds of another company	(12,000)	
Net cash from investing activities		$(14,000)

Cash from financing activities

Retired bonds payable	$(50,000)	
Made payment on loan	(3,400)	
Issued common stock	100,000	
Sold treasury stock	10,000	
Paid dividends	(40,000)	
Net cash from financing activities		$ 16,600

* An $80,000 building was purchased by making an $8,000 down payment and signing a 20-year mortgage note for the remainder.

4. Analysts interpret positive net cash from operating activities as a signal for positive future growth. Thus, management may be pressured into acting unethically and misclassifying cash inflows from investing or financing activities as cash inflows from operating activities. Management could also create positive cash from operating activities by misclassifying operating cash outflows as investing or financing activities.

CHAPTER 10
USING FINANCIAL STATEMENT ANALYSIS TO EVALUATE FIRM PERFORMANCE

Chapter Overview

This chapter introduces accounting for two new items that are sometimes found on the income statement. Techniques for analyzing financial statements are illustrated and discussed as well. Vertical and horizontal analyses are introduced, and ratios that were presented in previous chapters are revisited. Two new cash flow ratios and two new market indicator ratios are discussed.

Chapter Highlights

1. Because the earnings a company reports are so important, the Financial Accounting Standards Board (FASB) requires that two particular items be presented separately on the income statement and not be included with income from continuing operations. They are 1) discontinued operations, and 2) extraordinary items. Each of these is shown net of tax, that is, the tax expense or tax benefit is combined with the dollar amount of the gain or loss to show the after-tax effect of the item on earnings. You can remember the order in which they are presented by the letters **c-d-e**: income from **c**ontinuing operations, **d**iscontinued operations, and **e**xtraordinary items. If a company had both of these items, its income statement would look something like this:

> Revenues
> - Expenses
> Income before taxes
> - Income tax expense
> Income from continuing operations
> Discontinued operations:
> +/- Income or loss from discontinued operations, net of tax
> +/- Gain or loss on disposal, net of tax
> Income before extraordinary item
> +/- Extraordinary item, net of tax
> Net income

2. **Discontinued operations** are a part of a company's past activities that will not be

continued in the future. They represent a major portion of the business, usually a segment or an entire division, which will no longer earn profits (or incur losses) for the company. The actual disposal of the segment will happen only once and will not affect future earnings either, so the impact on income must be shown separately in the financial statements. Then analysts can better predict the company's future earnings.

If a company has discontinued operations, the first part of its income statement will show revenue, expenses, and income taxes for continuing operations. Then, under a heading called "discontinued operations," it will show the after-tax income or loss from operating the discontinued segment during the accounting period. A second line item, still under "discontinued operations," shows the after-tax gain or loss from the actual sale or disposal of the segment.

3. **Extraordinary items** are events that are both unusual in nature and infrequent in occurrence. Accountants must use professional judgment to decide if an item should be reported as extraordinary. Natural disasters, for example, will sometimes be considered extraordinary and sometimes not, depending upon how frequently they occur in a particular area. Other possible extraordinary items are the one-time cost of complying with new laws or the loss of assets in a foreign country seized by that country's government.

If any event qualifies as an extraordinary item, it will be shown on the income statement, net of tax, after income from continuing operations and any discontinued operations.

4. **Horizontal analysis** is a technique used to evaluate an individual financial statement line item over a period of time. A specific past year is chosen as a base year. The increase or decrease in the same line item for other years is then expressed as a percentage of the base year. For example:

Property, plant and equipment		
2010	2009	2008
$130,000	$120,000	$100,000
30%	20%	100%

In this example, 2008 is the base year. In 2009, PP&E has increased $20,000 ($120,000 minus $100,000). This $20,000 increase divided by the $100,000 base year equals 20%. During 2009, PP&E increased 20%. In 2010, PP&E was $30,000, or 30%, more than the base year of 2008.

This is only one way to do horizontal analysis. Sometimes the analyst simply compares each year with the previous year, rather than with a common base year:

Property, plant and equipment		
2010	2009	2008
$130,000	$120,000	$100,000
8%	20%	100%

In this example, PP&E in 2009 is still $20,000 (or 20%) more than it was in 2008. However, PP&E in 2010 is $10,000 more than in 2009, an 8% increase over the $120,000 of PP&E in 2009 ($10,000 divided by $120,000).

5. **Vertical analysis** expresses each line item on a particular year's financial statement as a percentage of a single item on that financial statement. The most common vertical analysis is performed on the income statement, where each line item on the statement is expressed as a percentage of sales for the period. This technique is more useful if two or more periods are available for comparison.

6. Ratio analysis uses information on the financial statements to calculate specific values, which can then be used to determine a company's financial condition. Ratios for a particular accounting period are more useful when compared with: 1) ratios from other periods, 2) industry averages, or 3) other companies in the same industry. Chapter 10 summarizes the ratios discussed in previous chapters and introduces a few new ratios as well.

Some analysts will use variations of the formulas presented in this book.

7. **Liquidity ratios** measure a firm's ability to meet its short-term debt obligations when they fall due.

- The **current ratio** measures a company's ability to cover its current liabilities (due within the next year) with its current assets, which are cash and items that will be converted into cash or used in the business during the next year. The current ratio is calculated as:

$$\frac{\text{Total current assets}}{\text{Total current liabilities}}$$

- The **quick ratio** (also called the **acid-test ratio**) is similar to the current ratio, but it is a tougher test of a company's short-term debt-paying ability. The numerator uses only the most liquid current assets: cash, short-term investments, and net accounts receivable. Since inventory must first be sold, and the related account receivable must then be collected, it is two steps away from cash and it is not used in the acid-test ratio. The formula is:

$$\frac{\text{Cash} + \text{Short-term investments} + \text{Net accounts receivable}}{\text{Total current liabilities}}$$

- **Working capital**, current assets minus current liabilities, is not actually a ratio, but it too is an indication of a company's ability to pay its short-term debts. It should be a positive number. If it is negative, a company's current liabilities are larger than its current assets and it will probably have trouble paying its short-term debts.

- The **inventory turnover ratio** measures how quickly a company turns over (or sells) its inventory. It is calculated as:

$$\frac{\text{Cost of goods sold}}{\text{Average inventory}}$$

- The **accounts receivable turnover ratio** measures how quickly a company turns over (or collects) its accounts receivable. It is calculated as:

$$\frac{\text{Net credit sales}}{\text{Average net accounts receivable}}$$

8. **Solvency ratios** are a measure of a company's ability to pay its long-term obligations and survive over time.

- The **debt to equity ratio** shows how much of a company's financing is provided by creditors and how much is provided by owners. The formula is:

$$\frac{\text{Total liabilities}}{\text{Total shareholders' equity}}$$

- **Times interest earned** shows how easily a company can handle the debt it already has. It compares a company's earnings with its interest:

$$\frac{\text{Income from operations}}{\text{Interest expense}}$$

9. **Profitability ratios** evaluate a company's earnings for a period of time.

- **Return on assets** compares a company's earnings with the assets invested to generate those earnings:

$$\frac{\text{Net income + interest expense}}{\text{Average total assets}}$$

- The **asset turnover ratio** measures how efficiently a company uses its assets:

$$\frac{\text{Net sales}}{\text{Average total assets}}$$

- **Return on equity** compares a company's earnings with the investment made by the common shareholders:

$$\frac{\text{Net income − preferred dividends}}{\text{Average common shareholders' equity}}$$

- The **gross profit ratio** measures the percentage of each dollar of sales that is left over after covering the cost of the merchandise:

$$\frac{\text{Gross profit}}{\text{Net sales}}$$

A small decrease in the gross profit percentage can make a big difference in a company's profitability.

- **Earnings per share** expresses the company's income on a per-share basis:

$$\frac{\text{Net income − preferred dividends}}{\substack{\text{Weighted average number of shares of} \\ \text{common stock outstanding}}}$$

10. Two new **market indicators**, presented for the first time in Chapter 10, are of interest to shareholders because they look at the current market price of the stock, which is the amount a new investor would pay for a share.

- The **price-earnings ratio** compares the market price of a share of stock with the earnings that share generates:

$$\frac{\text{Market price per common share}}{\text{Earnings per share}}$$

A high price-earnings ratio shows that investors believe the company has potential for future growth. However, it can also be an indicator of an over-valued stock.

- The **dividend yield** ratio compares the dividend paid on a single share of stock with the market price of that share:

$$\frac{\text{Dividend per share}}{\text{Market price per share}}$$

Dividend yields may be quite low, since many investors expect to profit from increases in the market price of the stock rather than dividends. However, some investors are dependent on dividend income and prefer stocks with a high dividend yield.

11. To minimize the risk of investing in stock, you should either find a financial advisor or become an expert from your own study and analysis of stocks. You also need to understand financial accounting and financial statement analysis. Investors should diversify, or invest in a variety of stocks, so that losses in one stock are offset by gains in another. A diversified portfolio, or group of investments, allows shareholders to minimize (but not eliminate) risk.

12. (Appendix A) There are several events that have a direct effect on owners' equity that are not reported on the income statement. Two of them are owner contributions (which increase contributed capital) and dividends to corporate owners (which decrease retained earnings). However, there are two other items, known as part of **other comprehensive income**, which are not shown on the income statement because they do not really reflect a firm's performance. The first item is unrealized gains and losses from foreign currency translations and the second is unrealized gains and losses on certain types of investments. Neither of these items appears on the income statement. Both of them are treated as direct additions to (if gains) or subtractions from (if losses) retained earnings. However, so that financial statement users will not overlook these items, the FASB requires that companies show **comprehensive income**, which is equal to net income (shown on the income statement) plus other comprehensive income. Comprehensive income, then, is the total of all items that affect shareholders' equity except for transactions with shareholders (such as issuing or repurchasing the company's stock or declaring dividends).

13. (Appendix B) Companies will often invest surplus cash in the stocks and bonds of other companies. Management's plans to sell or hold these securities determine how they should be treated.

- **Held-to-maturity securities** are debt securities that the company plans to keep until they mature. Equity securities (stocks) cannot be held-to-maturity securities because they do not have maturity dates. These debt securities are recorded at cost and shown as assets on the balance sheet at historical cost, (plus any unamortized premium or minus any unamortized discount). Changes in market value do not affect the recorded value of held-to-maturity securities.

- **Trading securities** are either debt or equity securities that the company has purchased in hope of making a short-term profit. These securities are first recorded at cost. However, before the company issues financial statements, it must revalue these securities and show them as current assets on the balance sheet at their market values, known as marking-to-market. If the market value is higher than cost, the company has an **unrealized gain**, (holding gain) and if the market value is lower than cost, the company has an **unrealized loss** (holding loss). Unrealized gains and losses on trading securities appear on the company's income statement.

- **Available-for-sale securities** are either debt or equity securities that the company does not plan to sell in the short-run, but does not intend to hold to maturity, either. These securities are initially recorded at cost and revalued to market value at the balance sheet date. Any unrealized gain or loss does not appear on the income statement, however. Instead, it is shown after retained earnings in the shareholders' equity section of the balance sheet. Unrealized gains and losses on available-for-sale securities are part of other comprehensive income.

Featured Exercise

Virtual Company
Consolidated Balance Sheet
At December 31,

millions, except share data	2009	2008	2007
Current assets			
Cash and cash equivalents	$ 5.6	$ 16.2	$ 14.9
Accounts receivable, less allowances	18.9	17.5	20.4
Inventories	32.4	39.4	38.6
Other current assets	3.8	1.2	2.3
Total current assets	60.7	74.3	76.2
Property, plant & equipment, net	145.7	135.8	122.4
Other assets	1.4	2.1	1.1
Total assets	207.8	212.2	199.7
Current liabilities			
Accounts payable	2.5	13.4	15.2
Current portion of long-term debt	24.3	22.9	21.5
Other current liabilities	1.9	2.1	0.7
Total current liabilities	28.7	38.4	37.4
Long-term debt	126.0	118.6	115.8
Other liabilities	1.6	1.4	1.2
Shareholders' equity			
Common stock, $0.10 par, 20,000,000 shares authorized			
Issued 14,000,000 shares in 2009, 13,700,000 in 2008			
and 13,650,000 in 2007	1.4	1.4	1.4
Capital in excess of par value	36.3	35.2	34.7
Retained earnings	25.9	22.1	18.7
Treasury stock at cost	(9.7)	(8.2)	(7.8)
Currency translation adjustment	(1.5)	1.9	(1.3)
Unrealized gain (loss) on available-for-sale securities	(0.9)	1.4	(0.4)
Total shareholders' equity	51.5	53.8	45.3
Total liabilities and shareholders' equity	$ 207.8	$ 212.2	$ 199.7

Virtual Company
Consolidated Statement of Earnings
For the Year Ended December 31,

millions, except share data	2009	2008	2007
Net sales	$ 120.8	$ 140.4	$ 109.5
Cost of goods sold	65.7	82.5	58.3
Selling and administrative expense	39.7	37.3	32.8
Operating profit	15.4	20.6	18.4
Interest expense	1.1	0.7	1.0
Earnings before income taxes	14.3	19.9	17.4
Income taxes	5.0	7.0	6.1
Net earnings	$ 9.3	$ 12.9	$ 11.3

Part A: Use the financial statements for Virtual Company to complete the ratios in the chart below. If you cannot calculate a ratio, explain why. The following additional information may be helpful:

	2009	2008	2007
Market price per share	$9.00	$13.00	$12.80
Dividend per common share	$0.60	$0.60	$0.58
Weighted average number of common shares outstanding during the year	13,800,000	13,680,000	13,600,000

		2009	2008	2007
1	Current ratio			
2	Quick ratio (acid-test ratio)			
3	Working capital			
4	Inventory turnover ratio			
5	Accounts receivable turnover ratio			
6	Debt to equity ratio			
7	Times interest earned ratio			
8	Return on assets			
9	Asset turnover ratio			
10	Return on equity			
11	Gross profit ratio			
12	Earnings per share			
13	Price-earnings ratio			
14	Dividend yield ratio			

Part B: Prepare a vertical analysis of Virtual Company's income statements for all three years.

	2009		2008		2007	
Net sales	$ 120.8		$ 140.4		$ 109.5	
Cost of goods sold	65.7		82.5		58.3	
Selling and administrative expense	39.7		37.3		32.8	
Operating profit	15.4		20.6		18.4	
Interest expense	1.1		0.7		1.0	
Earnings before income taxes	14.3		19.9		17.4	
Income taxes	5.0		7.0		6.1	
Net earnings	$ 9.3		$ 12.9		$ 11.3	

Part C: Prepare a horizontal analysis of the following selected items for Virtual Company. Use 2007 as the base year.

1		2009	2008	2007
	Accounts receivable	$18.9	$17.5	$20.4

2		2009	2008	2007
	Property, plant & equipment, net	$145.7	$135.8	$122.4

3		2009	2008	2007
	Net sales	$120.8	$140.4	$109.5

4		2009	2008	2007
	Net earnings	$9.3	$12.9	$11.3

Part D: (Appendix A) Use the financial statements for Virtual Company to complete the following chart:

		2009	2008	2007
1	Net income			

2	Other comprehensive income			
3	Comprehensive income			

Solution

Part A:		2009	2008	2007
1	Current ratio	$\dfrac{\$60.7}{\$28.7} = 2.11$	$\dfrac{\$74.3}{\$38.4} = 1.93$	$\dfrac{\$76.2}{\$37.4} = 2.04$
2	Quick ratio (acid-test ratio)	$\dfrac{\$5.6 + 18.9}{\$28.7} = .85$	$\dfrac{\$16.2 + 17.5}{\$38.4} = .88$	$\dfrac{\$14.9 + 20.4}{\$37.4} = .94$
3	Working capital	$\$60.7 - 28.7 = \$32.0$	$\$74.3 - 38.4 = \$35.9$	$\$76.2 - 37.4 = \$38.8$
4	Inventory turnover ratio	$\dfrac{\$65.7}{(\$32.4+39.4)/2} = 1.8$	$\dfrac{\$82.5}{(\$39.4+38.6)/2} = 2.1$	*Can't calculate average inventory for 2007*
5	Accounts receivable turnover ratio	$\dfrac{\$120.8}{(\$18.9+17.5)/2} = 6.6$	$\dfrac{\$140.4}{(\$17.5+20.4)/2} = 7.4$	*Can't calculate average A/R for 2007*
6	Debt to equity ratio	$\dfrac{\$28.7+126.0+1.6}{\$51.5} = 3.0$	$\dfrac{\$38.4+118.6+1.4}{\$53.8} = 2.9$	$\dfrac{\$37.4+115.8+1.2}{\$45.3} = 3.4$
7	Times interest earned	$\dfrac{\$9.3 + 1.1}{\$1.1} = 9.5$	$\dfrac{\$12.9 + 0.7}{\$0.7} = 19.4$	$\dfrac{\$11.3 + 1.0}{\$1.0} = 12.3$
8	Return on assets	$\dfrac{\$9.3 + 1.1}{(\$207.8 + 212.2)/2} =$ $0.0495 = 5\%$	$\dfrac{\$12.9 + 0.7}{(\$212.2 + 199.7)/2} =$ $.066 = 6.6\%$	*Can't calculate average assets for 2007*
9	Asset turnover ratio	$\dfrac{\$120.8}{(\$207.8 + 212.2)/2} =$ $.575$ times	$\dfrac{\$140.4}{(\$212.2 + 199.7)/2} =$ $.682$ times	*Can't calculate average assets for 2007*
10	Return on equity	$\dfrac{\$9.3 - 0}{(\$51.5 + 53.8)/2} =$ $0.177 = 17.7\%$	$\dfrac{\$12.9 - 0}{(\$53.8 + 45.3)/2} =$ $0.260 = 26.0\%$	*Can't calculate average shareholders' equity for 2007*
11	Gross profit ratio	$\dfrac{\$120.8-65.7}{\$120.8} = 45.6\%$	$\dfrac{\$140.4-82.5}{\$140.4} = 41.2\%$	$\dfrac{\$109.5-58.3}{\$109.5} = 46.8\%$
12	Earnings per share	$\dfrac{\$9,300,000}{13,800,000} = \$0.67$	$\dfrac{\$12,900,000}{13,680,000} = \$0.94$	$\dfrac{\$11,300,000}{13,600,000} = \$0.83$
13	Price-earnings ratio	$\dfrac{\$9.00}{\$0.67} = 13.4$	$\dfrac{\$13.00}{\$0.94} = 13.8$	$\dfrac{\$12.80}{\$0.83} = 15.4$
14	Dividend yield ratio	$\dfrac{\$0.60}{\$9.00} = .067 = 6.7\%$	$\dfrac{\$0.60}{\$13.00} = .046 = 4.6\%$	$\dfrac{\$0.58}{\$12.80} = .045 = 4.5\%$

Part B:	2009		2008		2007	
Net sales	$ 120.8	100.0%	$ 140.4	100.0%	$ 109.5	100.0%
Cost of goods sold	65.7	54.4%	82.5	58.8%	58.3	53.2%
Selling and admin. expense	39.7	32.9%	37.3	26.6%	32.8	30.0%
Operating profit	15.4	12.7%	20.6	14.7%	18.4	16.8%
Interest expense	1.1	0.9%	0.7	0.5%	1.0	0.9%
Earnings before income taxes	14.3	11.8%	19.9	14.2%	17.4	15.9%
Income taxes	5.0	4.1%	7.0	5.0%	6.1	5.6%
Net earnings	$ 9.3	7.7%	$ 12.9	9.2%	$ 11.3	10.3%

Part C:		2009	2008	2007
a	Accounts receivable	$18.9	$17.5	$20.4
		$\dfrac{\$18.9 - 20.4}{\$20.4} = (7.4)\%$	$\dfrac{\$17.5 - 20.4}{\$20.4} = (14.2)\%$	100%
b	Property, plant & equipment, net	$145.7	$135.8	$122.4
		$\dfrac{\$145.7 - 122.4}{\$122.4} = 19.0\%$	$\dfrac{\$135.8 - 122.4}{\$122.4} = 10.9\%$	100%
c	Net sales	$120.8	$140.4	$109.5
		$\dfrac{\$120.8 - 109.5}{\$109.5} = 10.3\%$	$\dfrac{\$140.4 - 109.5}{\$109.5} = 28.2\%$	100%
d	Net earnings	$9.3	$12.9	$11.3
		$\dfrac{\$9.3 - 11.3}{\$11.3} = -17.7\%$	$\dfrac{\$12.9 - 11.3}{\$11.3} = 14.2\%$	100%

Part D (Appendix A)		2009	2008	2007
1	Net income *Net income is the same as net earnings.*	$9.3	$12.9	$11.3
2	Other comprehensive income *unrealized gains & losses from foreign currency translation + unrealized gains & losses from available-for-sale securities*	$ (1.5) loss + (0.9) loss $ (2.4) loss	$ 1.9 gain + 1.4 gain $ 3.3 gain	$ (1.3) loss + (0.4) loss $ (1.7) loss
3	Comprehensive income *net income + other comprehensive income*	$9.3 – 2.4 = $6.9	$12.9 + 3.3 = $16.2	$11.3 – 1.7 = $9.6

Review Questions and Exercises

Completion Statements

Fill in the blank(s) to complete each statement.

1. _____ are events that are both unusual in nature and infrequent in occurrence.

2. _____ measures the percentage of each dollar of sales that is left over after covering the cost of the merchandise.

3. The _____ ratio shows how much of a company's financing is provided by creditors and how much is provided by owners.

4. _____ are a part of a company's past activities that will not be continued in the future.

5. _____ expresses each item on a particular year's financial statement as a percentage of a single item on that financial statement.

6. _____ is a technique used to evaluate an individual financial statement line item over a period of time. Often a specific past year is chosen as a base year.

7. _____ is the only ratio that companies are required to include with their financial statements. It appears on the _____.

8. To calculate the return on assets, you need two financial statements, the _____ and the _____.

9. (Appendix A) _____ is the total of all items that affect shareholders' equity except for transactions with shareholders.

10. (Appendix B) _____ are debt securities that the company plans to keep until they mature.

11. (Appendix B) _____ are either debt or equity securities that the company has purchased in hope of making a short-term profit.

12. (Appendix B) _____ are either debt or equity securities that the company does not plan to sell in the short-run, but does not intend to hold to maturity, either.

Solutions to Review Questions and Exercises

True/False

Indicate whether each statement is true (T) or false (F).

_____ 1. The current ratio will always be greater than 1.0.

_____ 2. The current ratio measures a company's solvency.

_____ 3. To prepare a vertical analysis of a company's income statement, you should divide each line item on the statement by total assets.

_____ 4. The asset turnover ratio is a measure of a company's profitability.

_____ 5. The accounts receivable turnover ratio is a measure of a company's profitability.

_____ 6. Ratios are more meaningful when they are compared with other companies in the same industry or with industry averages.

_____ 7. Investors should buy stocks with the highest possible price-earnings ratio.

_____ 8. Stock with a high dividend yield is a good investment.

_____ 9. To be classified as an extraordinary item, an event must be both unusual in nature and infrequent in occurrence.

_____ 10. Gains and losses from discontinued operations are shown separately on a company's income statement.

_____ 11. (Appendix A) Comprehensive income will always be greater than net income.

_____ 12. (Appendix B) Trading securities are shown on the balance sheet at historical cost.

_____ 13. (Appendix B) Held-to-maturity securities are shown on the balance sheet at historical cost, plus any unamortized premium minus any unamortized discount.

_____ 14. (Appendix B) Available-for-sale securities are shown on the balance sheet at historical cost.

Multiple Choice

Select the best answer for each question.

_____ 1. Beta Business has total current assets of $1,000,000 and total current liabilities of $400,000. Its current ratio is:
A. 2.00.
B. 2.25.
C. 2.50.
D. 0.40.

2. Beta Business has total current assets of $1,000,000 and total current liabilities of $400,000. If the company collects $100,000 of its accounts receivable, its current ratio will:
   A. increase.
   B. decrease.
   C. stay the same.
   D. The answer cannot be determined from the information given.

3. Beta Business has total current assets of $1,000,000 and total current liabilities of $400,000. If the company purchases $100,000 of inventory for cash, its quick ratio will:
   A. increase.
   B. decrease.
   C. stay the same.
   D. The answer cannot be determined from the information given.

4. Beta Business has total current assets of $1,000,000 and total current liabilities of $400,000. If the company purchases $100,000 of inventory and promises to pay for it in the next two weeks, its current ratio will:
   A. increase.
   B. decrease.
   C. stay the same.
   D. The answer cannot be determined from the information given.

5. Last year Iota, Inc. had earnings per share of $1.95. In December this year, Iota repurchased some of its own common stock. Assume that net income this year is the same as it was last year. This purchase of treasury stock will _____ the number of shares of common stock outstanding and _____ earnings per share.
   A. increase   increase
   B. increase   decrease
   C. decrease   decrease
   D. decrease   increase

6. Last year Madd Hatter, Inc., bought baseball caps for $3 each and sold them for $9. This year the company's supplier is charging $4 for each cap, but Madd Hatter cannot raise its prices because competition is too tough. If Madd Hatter continues to sell caps for $9, its gross profit per cap will _____ and its gross profit ratio will _____.
   A. increase   increase
   B. increase   decrease
   C. decrease   decrease
   D. decrease   increase

7. Nu News, Inc., has total current assets of $1,000,000 and total current liabilities of $500,000. If the company pays $100,000 of accounts payable, its current ratio will:
   A. increase.
   B. decrease.
   C. stay the same.
   D. The answer cannot be determined from the information given.

_____ 8. If a company increases its collection effort, it hopes to see its accounts receivable turnover ratio _____, because the average amount of accounts receivable will _____.
    A. increase   increase
    B. increase   decrease
    C. decrease   decrease
    D. decrease   increase

_____ 9. One of Caribbean Cruises' ships hit an iceberg just off Miami and sank. Icebergs in the Caribbean are both unusual and infrequent, so the company plans to treat the $10,000,000 uninsured loss as an extraordinary item. The company's tax rate is 35%. What effect will this event have on net income for the year?
    A. Net income will decrease $3,500,000.
    B. Net income will decrease $6,500,000.
    C. No effect. Extraordinary items appear on the balance sheet as a direct increase or decrease to retained earnings.
    D. No effect. Companies are not required to report extraordinary items because they will have no effect on future earnings.

_____ 10. Which of the following ratios would most interest a banker who is thinking about making a long-term loan to a company?
    A. Return on equity
    B. Return on assets
    C. Dividend yield
    D. Debt to equity

Exercises

1. Classify each of the ratios listed in the table below by putting an X in the appropriate box.

		Liquidity	Solvency	Profitability	Market indicator
a	Return on assets				
b	Times interest earned ratio				
c	Current ratio				
d	Return on equity				
e	Debt to equity ratio				
f	Working capital				
g	Gross profit ratio				
h	Accounts receivable turnover ratio				
i	Dividend yield ratio				
j	Inventory turnover ratio				
k	Quick ratio				
l	Earnings per share				
m	Price-earnings ratio				
n	Asset turnover ratio				

2. 2009 was a very eventful year for Buck's Better Bacon.
- Buck's decided to discontinue its manure processing division, which wasn't very profitable even in good years. On October 31, Buck's sold the division for a small gain of $10,000. Up to the date of sale, the division earned revenues of $50,000 and had expenses of $45,000.
- In August, an earthquake leveled Buck's Iowa research farm. Uninsured damages amounted to $300,000. Buck's will treat this disaster as an extraordinary loss, since earthquakes in Iowa are both unusual and infrequent.
- Normal continuing operations earned revenues of $900,000. Expenses were $600,000. Buck's has a 30% tax rate that applies to all income.

Prepare an income statement for the year ended December 31, 2009, in good form.

Buck's Better Bacon, Inc.
Income Statement
For the Year Ended December 31, 2009

Completion Statements

1. Extraordinary items
2. Gross profit ratio
3. debt to equity
4. Discontinued operations
5. Vertical analysis
6. Horizontal analysis
7. Earnings per share; income statement
8. income statement; balance sheet
9. (Appendix B) Held-to-maturity securities
10. (Appendix B) Trading securities
11. (Appendix B) Available-for-sale securities
12. (Appendix A) Comprehensive income

True/False

1. False   A company's current ratio will be greater than 1.0 only when its current assets are greater than its current liabilities.
2. False   The current ratio measures a company's liquidity.
3. False   Divide each line item on the income statement by net sales, not total assets.
4. True
5. False   The accounts receivable turnover ratio measures a company's liquidity.
6. True
7. False   Although a high price-earnings ratio may indicate that investors expect future growth, a high price-earnings ratio may also be the sign of an over-valued stock.
8. False   Some investors are dependent on dividend income and prefer stocks with a high dividend yield. However, many investors expect to profit from increases in the market price of the stock rather than dividends. For them, a low dividend yield is fine.
9. True
10. True
11. False   (Appendix A) Comprehensive income is net income plus other comprehensive income. The elements of other comprehensive income include losses as well as gains, so it's possible that comprehensive income will be smaller than net income.
12. False   (Appendix B) Trading securities are shown at their market value as of the balance sheet date.
13. True   (Appendix B)
14. False   (Appendix B) Available-for-sale securities are shown at their market value as of the balance sheet date.

Multiple Choice

1. C $1,000,000/$400,000 = 2.5
2. C   If Beta collects $100,000 of accounts receivable, its cash will increase $100,000 while its accounts receivable decrease $100,000. Total current assets will still be $1,000,000.
3. B   The quick ratio includes only cash, short-term investments, and accounts receivable in the numerator. Beta is decreasing cash with this purchase of inventory, so its acid-test ratio will decrease, even though its total current assets remain the same.
4. B   Both current assets and current liabilities increase by $100,000. $1,100,000/$500,000 = 2.2
5. D   Treasury stock is subtracted from shareholders' equity and reduces the number of shares held by those outside the company. With fewer shares outstanding, the denominator of the EPS calculation will be smaller, and earnings for each outstanding common share will be larger.

6. C   Last year the company's gross profit was $6 per cap, which is 67% of sales. This year, gross profit will be only $5 per cap, or 56%.

7. A   Right now the company's current ratio is $1,000,000/$500,000, or 2.0. If it pays $100,000 of accounts payable, both current assets and current liabilities will decrease by $100,000. $900,000/$400,000 = 2.25

8. B   If a company collects its receivables more quickly, fewer dollars will remain uncollected in accounts receivable at any given point in time. The denominator of the accounts receivable turnover ratio will decrease, which increases the ratio itself.

9. B. Extraordinary items appear on the income statement after discontinued operations. They are shown net of tax. The $10,000,000 loss will result in a tax savings of 35% times $10,000,000, or $3,500,000. The overall impact of the extraordinary loss is to reduce income by $10,000,000 – 3,500,000 = $6,500,000.

10. D   The debt to equity ratio compares the amount of debt financing the company already has to the amount of financing provided by its shareholders. A banker would look at this ratio to determine if a company could take on additional debt. The other ratios listed in this question are of more interest to shareholders than creditors.

Exercises

1.		Liquidity	Solvency	Profitability	Market indicator
a	Return on assets			X	
b	Times interest earned ratio		X		
c	Current ratio	X			
d	Return on equity			X	
e	Debt to equity ratio		X		
f	Working capital	X			
g	Gross profit ratio			X	
h	Accounts receivable turnover ratio	X			
i	Dividend yield ratio				X
j	Inventory turnover ratio	X			
k	Quick ratio	X			
l	Earnings per share			X	
m	Price-earnings ratio				X
n	Asset turnover ratio			X	

2.

Buck's Better Bacon, Inc.
Income Statement
For the Year Ended December 31, 2009

Revenues		$900,000
Expenses		600,000
Income before taxes		300,000
Income tax expense		90,000
Income from continuing operations		210,000
Discontinued operations		
Income from discontinued operations, net of $1,500 tax	$3,500 [1]	
Gain or loss on disposal, net of $3,000 tax	7,000 [2]	10,500
Income before extraordinary item		220,500
Extraordinary loss from earthquake, net of $90,000 tax savings [3]		(210,000)
Net income		$ 10,500

---

[1] Revenue	$50,000
Expenses	45,000
Income before tax	5,000
Taxes (30%)	1,500
Net income	$ 3,500

[2] $10,000 gain x 30% = $3,000 tax

[3] The loss is tax deductible, so Buck's will save 30% x $300,000, or $90,000 in taxes. The $300,000 loss decreases income, but the $90,000 saved in taxes increases income, so the overall effect on profits is a decrease of $210,000.

CHAPTER 11
QUALITY OF EARNINGS AND CORPORATE GOVERNANCE

Chapter Overview

In this chapter, you will learn about the significance of earnings per share and the common ways management may manipulate earnings. You will also learn about the importance of effective corporate governance and how the Sarbanes-Oxley Act of 2002 is designed to help prevent future corporate misconduct.

Chapter Highlights

1. When evaluating a firm's performance, investors focus heavily on earnings per share. If a company's earnings per share does not meet Wall Street's and financial analysts' expectations, the company's stock price will most likely fall. This creates pressure for management to manipulate earnings in order to meet expectations. Manipulation compromises the quality of earnings and raises concerns that earnings reported to the public may not truly reflect a company's performance.

2. Two accounting authors, Leopold Bernstein and John Wild (*2000 Analysis of Financial Statements),* say the quality of earnings is affected in three ways:

- Management's choice of accounting methods has an impact on the quality of earnings. Conservative choices, which report lower net income and lower assets or higher liabilities, tend to result in higher quality earnings. A conservative choice of inventory method, such as using LIFO rather than FIFO, leads to reporting higher cost of goods sold, and lower net income and total assets. A conservative treatment for depreciating long-term assets would be choosing shorter estimated useful lives or lower salvage values, because this results in higher depreciation expense for the year.

- The quality of earnings will be lower for companies that record revenues early and/or expenses late.

- The quality of earnings is also affected by the degree of risk a company faces. A company that faces fewer risks will tend to have higher quality earnings. The more risks a company faces the more likely management will feel pressure to manipulate earnings.

3. There are three accounting procedures used to **"cook the books,"** which means to manipulate or falsify financial statements to make the company's performance look better or worse than it truly is.

- **Big bath** charges occur in an accounting period when a company's earnings per share is going to fail to meet investors' expectations. The theory is that management will maximize its loss in that period by recording expenses that belong in future accounting periods and by writing off assets that may need to be written off in future periods. Management's goal is to make the already bad year worse so that future earnings will look better. To identify this type of manipulation, you should look for unusual amounts of expenses and write-offs in comparison with previous years. You should also read the notes to the financial statements and periodicals about the company.

- **Cookie jar reserves** involve the estimated reserve accounts, such as allowance for uncollectible accounts and estimated warranty liability. Management may increase or decrease these reserves in order to manipulate earnings. If this year's earnings are going to be higher than investors' expectations, than the incentive may be to smooth earnings by increasing the current period expenses. This provides a larger reserve, or cookie jar, to dip into in future periods when earnings may not be meeting investors' expectations. Ratio analyses of the company's reserve accounts and reading the notes to the financial statements may help to identify this type of manipulation.

- Management may also manipulate earnings by recognizing revenues either too early or too late. GAAP requires that revenues be recorded when the earnings process is complete and collection is reasonably assured. This rule is open to interpretation and thus is sometimes abused. Management abuses can range from recording revenues in the wrong accounting period to recording fictitious revenues. Reading the company's **revenue recognition** policy in the first note to the financial statements may help to identify these abuses. Ratio analyses such as accounts receivable to sales should also help to identify manipulation when the current year is compared with prior years.

4. Understanding the causes of the business failures of the past decade may help to prevent similar problems from occurring in the future. The over-reliance on earnings per share is part of the problem. Some executives manipulate earnings to bolster stock prices so they may benefit personally when selling their shares of the company's stock. Managements' use of estimates and interpretations of accounting rules must be better disclosed in the financial statements. The tone at the top has a large impact on the behavior of other employees in the company. The executives or top management must establish ethical behavior and demand it from others in the company. Auditors have to be independent of their clients so they can be objective in performing audits. Steps to address these problems and issues should help reduce fraud, although there is no way for accounting rules to completely stop fraud.

5. The **Sarbanes-Oxley Act** of 2002 (SOX) was enacted in response to the scandals and financial debacles of the early 2000's. The aim of the new regulation is to improve corporate governance. **Corporate governance** is the way a company governs itself and interacts with its board of directors, management, shareholders, auditors, and any others with a stake in the company. SOX directly affects the following groups:

- Management is now required to include in the annual report a report on the company's internal controls. The external auditors must attest to the accuracy of this report. The CEO and the CFO now must certify that they have reviewed the annual financial statements and swear that they are aware of no false statements or omissions. Management must provide a way, including a hotline, to report anonymously any fraudulent activity in the company. Management is not allowed to punish an employee for disclosing suspected fraud (whistle-blowing).

- The board of directors (BOD), elected by the shareholders to represent their interests, has an audit committee that oversees the company's financial matters. SOX requires that this audit committee be independent and have no members who are company managers. The audit committee is responsible for hiring, compensating and overseeing the work of the company's external auditors (public accounting firm).

- External auditors are hired by the audit committee of the company's BOD and provide an opinion on whether the firm's financial statements fairly present the company's financial position and the results of operations in accordance with GAAP. SOX requires that the external auditors be independent of their clients and prohibits the auditors from also performing consulting services. The auditors are now required to report directly to the audit committee and not to the company's management team.

- The Public Company Accounting Oversight Board (PCAOB) was newly formed to regulate the auditing profession. The SEC appoints the members and approves all its rules. All publicly traded companies are required to follow PCAOB rules.

6. It is difficult to measure the quality of and improvement in corporate governance. Steven Baum, chairman, president, and CEO of Sempra Energy ("Ask the CEO," *Business Week Online,* May 6, 2003), suggests good corporate governance includes the following:

- Highly qualified, experienced directors on the board who are independent of management

- Review of major management and financial decisions by the board of directors

- Transparent, easy-to-follow financial information for the shareholders

- Incentive-based compensation plans for management that lead to increased shareholder wealth, not just an increase in the stock price for the immediate future

- Independent, ethical auditors

To assess the quality of corporate governance, more investors are using rating systems provided by such companies as Moody's and others. Investors can also check companies' Web sites for corporate governance policies. Another indication of a company's quality of corporate governance is the report on a company's internal control system and the results of the external auditors' review of the system.

Featured Exercise

Part A: Identify whether each of the following will make earnings per share higher, lower, or not affected by putting an X in the correct column.

	Krupt, Inc.:	Higher	Lower	Not affected
1.	included in its sales for the year the goods that were delivered FOB destination at year-end but had not yet arrived at the buyer's place of business.			
2.	included in inventory the goods that were purchased FOB shipping point at year-end but had not yet arrived.			
3.	recorded the repair of its trucks as capital expenditures.			
4.	estimated the useful lives of the majority of its long-term assets to be five years when the industry average is more like ten years.			
5.	repurchased 40% of its shares outstanding at year-end in order to inflate the price of its stock.			

Part B: For each of the following, identify whether Krupt, Inc.'s manipulations are considered "Big Bath Charges", "Cookie Jar Reserve", and/or "Revenue Recognition" manipulations. There can be more than one correct answer for each.

	Krupt, Inc.:	Big Bath Charges	Cookie Jar Reserve	Revenue Recognition
1.	included in its sales for the year the goods that were delivered FOB destination at year-end but had not yet arrived at the buyer's place of business.			
2.	overstated its bad debts expense.			
3.	recorded many capital expenditures as revenue expenditures.			
4.	underestimated its warranty expense.			
5.	wrote off 30% of its intangible assets, which were still considered to have future economic benefit.			

Part C: Describe the new responsibilities or changes required by SOX for each of the following groups:

1. Management:

2. Board of directors:

3. External auditors:

4. Public Company Accounting Oversight Board:

Solution

Part A:

	Krupt, Inc.:	Higher	Lower	Not affected
1.	included in its sales for the year the goods that were delivered FOB destination at year-end but had not yet arrived at the buyer's place of business.	X		
2.	included in inventory the goods that were purchased FOB shipping point at year-end but had not yet arrived.			X
3.	recorded the repair of its trucks as capital expenditures.	X		
4.	estimated the useful lives of the majority of its long-term assets to be five years when the industry average is more like ten years.		X	
5.	repurchased 40% of its shares outstanding at year-end in order to inflate the price of its stock.	X		

Part B:

	Krupt, Inc.:	Big Bath Charges	Cookie Jar Reserve	Revenue Recognition
1.	included in its sales for the year the goods that were delivered FOB destination at year-end but had not yet arrived at the buyer's place of business.			X
2.	overstated its bad debts expense.	X	X	
3.	recorded many capital expenditures as revenue expenditures.	X		
4.	underestimated its warranty expense.		X	
5.	wrote off 30% of its intangible assets, which were still considered to have future economic benefit.	X		

Part C:
1. Management must report on the internal controls. The CEO and CFO must certify that they are unaware of any false statements in or omissions from the annual financial statements. They must provide means for anonymous reporting of fraudulent activity.
2. The board of directors is required to have an audit committee of independent directors, which cannot include company management.
3. The external auditors must be independent of and not perform consulting services for their clients. They must report directly to the audit committee and not to the company's managers.
4. The PCAOB was newly formed to regulate the auditing profession.

Review Questions and Exercises

Completion Statements

Fill in the blank(s) to complete each statement.

1. _____ _____ _____ is net income divided by the weighted average number of outstanding shares of (common) stock.

2. _____ the _____ is a slang term that means to manipulate or falsify the firm's accounting records to make the firm's financial performance or position look better than it actually is.

3. The _____ _____ theory is the type of manipulation where management maximizes a current loss to get rid of expenses that belong on future years' income statements.

4. The term for manipulating earnings by misstating reserves such as the allowance for uncollectible accounts is called _____ _____ reserves.

5. _____ _____ describes how a firm governs itself and is executed by the board of directors.

True/False

Indicate whether each statement is true (T) or false (F).

_____ 1. External auditors are required to audit all publicly-traded companies' internal control systems and write an opinion which is to be included with each company's annual report.

_____ 2. The cookie jar reserve is a term used to describe the manipulation of earnings by misstating allowance and/or reserve accounts.

_____ 3. The quality of earnings per share is improved when a company chooses an inventory method that results in a lower cost of goods sold.

_____ 4. The SOX Act requires external auditors to report directly to management to avoid any miscommunication.

_____ 5. The purpose of the PCAOB is to regulate the auditing profession.

Multiple Choice

_____ 1. Which of the following may indicate a company is manipulating earnings using big bath charges?
   A. Higher than usual revenues for the year
   B. Higher than usual expenses for the year
   C. Lower than usual allowance for uncollectible accounts at year-end
   D. Lower than usual payables at year-end

2. Which of the following is a new requirement imposed by the SOX Act?
   A. The CFO must be part of the audit committee.
   B. The external auditors must oversee the PCAOB.
   C. Management is required to have external auditors assess and give an opinion as to the effectiveness of the company's internal control system.
   D. All of the above are new requirements.

3. The quality of earnings is considered to be higher if:
   A. management chooses the conservative methods of accounting.
   B. the level of internal and external risks of the company is higher.
   C. the revenues are recognized early or expenses are postponed to a later period.
   D. All of the above will lead to higher quality of earnings.

4. Which of the following is an indication of good corporate governance?
   A. Boards of directors are independent of management.
   B. Boards of directors are involved in major management and financial decisions.
   C. Financial statements are transparent.
   D. All of the above are indicators.

5. The SOX Act now requires external auditors to:
   A. no longer provide information processing consulting services to their audit clients.
   B. assess and give an opinion on the effectiveness of the board of directors.
   C. be paid by the PCAOB instead of their audit clients in order to strength independence.
   D. be on the client's board of directors.

USE THE FOLLOWING INFORMATION TO ANSWER THE NEXT TWO QUESTIONS:
This month Tom's Wear tried calculating its bad debts expense two different ways. Using a percentage of credit sales, bad debts expense would be $1,500. Based on an aging of accounts receivable, however, bad debts expense would be $1,750.

6. If Tom's Wear decides to report $1,750 of bad debts expense, this accounting choice would be considered:
   A. conservative.
   B. fundamental.
   C. basic.
   D. aggressive.

7. If Tom's Wear decides to report $1,500 of bad debts expense, this accounting choice would be considered:
   A. conservative.
   B. fundamental.
   C. basic.
   D. aggressive.

8. Who is ultimately responsible for the accuracy of a company's financial statements?
   A. management
   B. the board of directors
   C. the external auditors
   D. the PCAOB

_____ 9. Who is responsible for giving an opinion on whether or not a company's financial statements fairly present the company's financial position and results of operations?
   A. management
   B. the board of directors
   C. the external auditors
   D. the PCAOB

Exercises

1. Put an X in the appropriate box to identify each of the following as either overstating, understating or not affecting earnings per share:

		Overstating	Understating	Not affecting
a.	Recorded capital expenditures as revenue expenditures			
b.	Depreciated land			
c.	Overstated the allowance for uncollectible accounts			
d.	Reported a current liability as a long-term liability			
e.	Paid a cash dividend to all shares outstanding			

2. Match each group with its new responsibilities required by the SOX Act.

_____ Management

_____ Board of directors

_____ External auditors

_____ PCAOB

A. Reports directly to the audit committee, not the executives

B. Members are appointed by the SEC

C. Includes an audit committee independent of company executives

D. Must provide a mechanism for anonymous reporting of fraudulent activities.

3. Ace Electronics just spent $200,000 to buy forty new electronic cash registers for its chain of stores. Due to rapid changes in technology, Ace expects to use these cash registers for four or five years, after which they will be worthless because they are obsolete.

   a. How much depreciation expense will Ace record each year using the straight-line method and an estimated useful life of four years?

   b. How much depreciation expense will Ace record each year using the straight-line method and an estimated useful life of five years?

   c. If Ace has 1,000,000 weighted-average shares of common stock outstanding, how much difference will the choice of useful life make in the company's earnings per share?

d. Which useful life would be considered aggressive? _____

e. Which useful life would improve the quality of Acme's earnings? _____

Solutions to Review Questions and Exercises

Completion Statements
1. Earnings per share
2. Cooking (the) books
3. big bath
4. cookie jar
5. Corporate governance

True/False

1. True
2. True
3. False   The quality of earnings improves when a company chooses the more conservative method, which yields lower net income and total assets. The inventory method that results in a lower cost of goods sold and higher reported net income is not conservative.
4. False   The external auditors must report directly to the audit committee and board of directors, not management.
5. True

Multiple Choice

1. B   Big bath charges maximize an already losing company's losses in that period by recording expenses that belong in future accounting periods and writing off assets that may need to be written off in future periods. A. is incorrect because big bath charges relate to overstating expenses, not revenues. C. is wrong because manipulating allowances (or reserves) downward results in expenses being understated, not overstated. D. is incorrect because payables would be overstated, not understated.
2. C   A. is wrong because the audit committee must be independent of management in order to ensure objectivity. B. is incorrect because the PCAOB oversees the external auditors.
3. A   B. is incorrect because the higher the risks, the higher the potential for manipulated earnings. C. is incorrect because quality is diminished if revenues are overstated and expenses are understated.
4. D
5. A   B. is incorrect because the auditors report to, not on, the board of directors. C. is incorrect because the auditors are paid by their clients, not the PCAOB. D is incorrect because the auditors must be independent of their clients.
6. A   If Tom's Wear reports higher bad debts expense, then reported net income and total assets will be lower, which is a conservative choice.
7. D   If Tom's Wear reports lower bad debts expense, then reported net income and total assets will be higher, which is an aggressive choice.
8. A
9. C

Exercises

1.		Overstating	Understating	Not affecting
a.	Recorded capital expenditures as revenue expenditures		X	
b.	Depreciated land		X	
c.	Overstated the allowance for uncollectible accounts		X	
d.	Reported a current liability as a long-term liability			X
e.	Paid a cash dividend to all shares outstanding			X

2. Management: D.,   Board of directors: C.,   External auditors: A.,   PCAOB: B

3. a. ($200,000 – 0) / 4 years = $50,000
   b. ($200,000 – 0) / 5 years = $40,000
   c. (50,000 – 40,000) / 1,000,000 shares = $0.01 per share
   d. five years, because it leads to reporting lower expenses and higher income
   e. four years, because it leads to reporting higher expenses and lower income, so net income and total assets are less likely to be overstated